WRITING AT THE THRESHOLD

WRITING AT THE THRESHOLD

Featuring 56 Ways to Prepare High School and College Students to Think and Write at the College Level

LARRY WEINSTEIN
BENTLEY COLLEGE

National Council of Teachers of English
1111 W. Kenyon Road, Urbana, Illinois 61801-1096

Staff Editor: Tom Tiller

Interior Design: R. Maul

Cover Design: Diana Coe/ko Design Studio

Cover Image: ©Eyewire

NCTE Stock Number: 59133-3050

Grateful acknowledgment is made to the following parties for permission to reprint copyrighted material:

"The Red Wheelbarrow" by William Carlos Williams, from *Collected Poems: 1909–1939, Volume I,* copyright ©1938 by New Directions Publishing Corp. Reprinted by permission of New Directions Publishing Corp.

The painting "Tea Party with Bomber" is reprinted by permission of Emily Hiestand. ©1983 by Emily Hiestand.

Library of Congress Cataloging-in-Publication Data

Weinstein, Larry, 1948–

Writing at the threshold : featuring 56 ways to prepare high school and college students to think and write at the college level / Larry Weinstein.

p. cm.

Includes bibliographical references (p.).

ISBN 0-8141-5913-3 (pbk.)

1. English language—Rhetoric—Study and teaching. 2. English language—Composition and exercises—Study and teaching (Secondary) 3. Critical thinking—Study and teaching (Secondary) 4. Critical thinking—Study and teaching (Higher) 5. Report writing—Study and teaching (Secondary) 6. Report writing—Study and teaching (Higher) I. Title.

PE1404 .W44 2001
808′.042′0711—dc21

2001030462

To Diane

Acknowledgments

The many debts I have incurred while developing and testing my teaching ideas—and while writing them up in the form of this book—make a staggering sum.

Readers familiar with the works of Peter Elbow, William Perry, Mina Shaughnessy, and Eleanor Duckworth will, I suspect, have little trouble spotting traces of their influence throughout these pages, even if their names do not appear frequently. I have personally known only two of them, but they are all my benefactors.

In addition, I owe the existence of this book to many colleagues (at Harvard University and Bentley College), teachers at the high school level, former students, friends, and family members who have generously fed my understanding with their thoughts and counterthoughts over almost thirty years: Marion Bishop, Joan Bolker, Jonathan Bransfield, Jacqueline Chong, Dave Colozzi, Robert Crooks, Nancy Disenhaus, Evelyn Farbman, Dennis Flynn, Mike Frank, Kerry (O'Shea) Gorgone, Barbara Gottfried, Bruce Herzberg, Justin Hoskins, the late Richard Marius, Mo (McGrath) Neff, Sheila Reindl, Rob Riordan, Ruth Spack, Teresa Vilardi, Jennifer Wagnon, Noam Weinstein, Rachel Weinstein, and Brian Woodward.

Throughout revision of the book, I have relied on the extensive critical feedback of ten good people: Pierce Butler of my own department at Bentley College, Jean Chandler of the New England Conservatory, Zarina Hock at NCTE, Margaret Metzger of Brookline High School, Sally Parr of SUNY Cortland, Lowry Pei of Simmons College, Joan Soble of Cambridge Rindge and Latin School, Tom Tiller at NCTE, my wife Diane Weinstein, and my brother Warren Weinstein.

To every person mentioned above—as well as to the *un*named people who have aided and abetted me, who *would* be named here if my memory served better—thank you and again thank you. It seems to take a village to raise an author.

Finally, however, even heartfelt thanks are insufficient for one of the persons I have named. She was my book's first fan. She alone, of all those named, has had to live with me through every up and down that the project of a book has visited on me. She alone has known—with the extraordinary instinct of a deeply gifted counselor—how to sit through every one of my expressions of discouragement until the time was right to ask when I was getting back to work. (She knows who she is.)

Contents

Why This Book

"If at first you don't succeed. . . ."

Over a wonderfully rewarding twenty-eight years of teaching writing, I have, I fear, sometimes struck my colleagues as a kind of pedagogical mad scientist. I have tried teaching "from the sentence up"; I have tried assigning fine pieces of published prose as models to be imitated; I have tried letting students collectively generate their own criteria for judging writing (and evaluated students' papers using those criteria); I have tried interviewing twelve distinguished writers on the Harvard faculty and using my taped interviews with them instead of handbooks. . . . Even if—as turned out to be the case—none of these *specific* teaching methods served students well, I was bound, I felt, eventually to hit upon some things that worked.

Here, then, are the methods that have worked, as well as several ways to sequence those methods to create whole courses from them (the five course plans that appear at book's end). Occasionally you'll also notice a small computer icon that indicates a reference to my Web site, where I've placed a number of materials that can be printed out, copied, and distributed to students directly.

I hope that some ideas you encounter in this book prove useful to you. Knowing that colleagues in the field were appropriating innovations found here would—together with the benefits my students have derived—incline me to suppose that my long years in an obscure "classroom laboratory" have, after all, been well spent.

Having said that, however, let me now complicate this introduction. For as much as *Writing at the Threshold* is meant to be a good collection of discrete methods—yes, a "cookbook," if you will—it is meant also to be a statement of philosophy about composition instruction. What I needed back in 1973, when I embarked on my career as a writing teacher at the college level, is, it seems to me, what is still needed by teachers of writing today: not only a supply of effective teaching methods, but also a clear, well-considered formulation of the teacher's purposes. Accordingly, into this book of strategies and ploys I have inserted several short, relevant, and (I hope) stimulating essays on the proper aims of a teacher of writing.

Two of those aims subsume all the others: (a) the aim to tap—or set in motion—*every student's inborn ability to think extensively and well,* and (b) the aim to provide every student with the skills he or she will need in order to *communicate* good thinking, to obtain a *fair hearing* for it.

Put another way, the "threshold" to which I refer in this book's title is not just the one that leads from high school to college; it is that which, at any age, leads from doing slavish or derivative thinking to doing real, engaged thinking of one's own. It is also that which leads—eventually—to prose that is lucid and coherent even when its subject is elusive or complex.

It is, to my mind, the most important threshold that our students cross.

I. The Thinking That *Produces* Things to Say

Teaching Ideas 1–6: *Catching* Students Thinking

The vast majority of students are capable of more extensive and valuable thought than they display in the papers they write. When they write, students do not so much think as locate thoughts and serve them up, hoping that their offerings—unprocessed and, in consequence, simplistic though they are—will still suffice. The subtext of most students' prose does not read, "I've been doing some thinking on this subject and would like to tell you how it seems to me now"; it reads, "Is this okay? Will this do?"[1]

If I believed that students were not up for more—by "more" I mean true inquiry—perhaps I could content myself with such poor, derivative fare. Perhaps, as I picked up my paycheck, I could tell myself that I am involved in the honorable work of taking human beings whose native intelligence does not approach my own and preparing them for decent lives even so. By teaching them some paragraph coherence and placement of commas, I would be preserving them from shame in their jobs and their communities, and that would be enough.

But they *are* capable of more. As I shall briefly try to show below, cognitive psychology tells us that, just as common experience tells us that.

Writers on cognition may differ from one another in the terms they use (for example, Dewey's "certain acquired habitual modes of understanding" become "sets" in Thorndike, "schemata" in Piaget), but through their diverse terms there emerges an outline of the process of human inquiry from which few of them dissent significantly:

1. The thinker is confronted with a situation that raises a question.
2. The thinker taps memory for relevant ideas or experiences and, on finding some, generates a possible answer to the question.
3. The thinker takes that answer and tests it, asking, "Does it, in fact, account for the scene at hand?"
4. If the mind's first answer fills the bill, the thinker stops inquiring quite soon. If, however, the mind's initial hypothesis fails to survive this test—or if it survives, but other plausible hypotheses have yet to be tested—the diligent thinker plunges on, posing and testing alternative hypotheses until one does survive the test or the thinker exhausts available hypotheses and means of testing.[2]

The sound of focused thought—the purposeful tussle of hypotheses and facts—is unmistakable. Here, for example, is the opening of an essay by a student of mine asked to interpret statistical results of a survey of all students in Expository Writing:

> I am considering the following statistic. Out of 689 students reacting to the statement "My Expos class is better than most other Expos classes":
> 35.7% strongly agreed,
> 22.5% agreed,
> 20.5% were unsure,
> 10.4% disagreed, and
> 10.9% strongly disagreed with the statement.
> My first reaction to the statistic is quite positive: Most of the students' Expos classes are better than most of the students' Expos classes.

Student X's very next word is "What?" He does a double-take. He sees that the statistic he has started to ponder cannot possibly mean what it first appears to mean; a minority of a population can have something "better than most" have, but a majority cannot. Frankly puzzled, Student X proceeds to give the original survey statement a second, closer reading: "My Expos class is better than most other Expos classes." "Classes." A second possible interpretation of the statistic occurs to him: "that most of the students were in a minority of larger, better classes." This would explain how most classes were inferior while the majority of students were enrolled in superior classes. But Student X rejects this, his second interpretation, as well, and moves on to entertain other, more plausible explanations, until he has obtained one that more or less satisfies him.

Is such mental work beyond the range of all but a select few?

The majority of cognitive psychologists resoundingly answer, "No." Nonpsychologists would, no doubt, also answer, "No." It takes no special expertise to spot the exercise of common reason.

By way of showing how natural a procedure inquiry is, John Dewey's classic *How We Think*, a very lucid presentation of essentially the same model sketched above, offers several good, real examples of thought drawn from "extracurricular" life, such as a certain student's actual (reported) sequence of thought when he saw that he was running late for an appointment and sought ways to make up for lost time (1991, 68–69).

Dewey might well have filled his whole book with such examples of inquiry. One inquires in deciding what clothes to put on in the morning "where in the world" one has left one's keys, what physiological and/or environmental conditions have given one cold-like symptoms, whether one's boss's comment on one's job performance was meant as a joke—and so forth and so on, all day long.

When the inquiry involved on such occasions is spelled out, some permutation of the basic model invariably emerges. Again . . .

1. *The thinker is confronted with a situation that raises a question.* Say that a friend passes you on the street and you greet her, but she does not return your greeting. The question raised is, "Why didn't Samantha say hello?"
2. *The thinker's mind goes to memory for relevant ideas or experiences and, sensing it has found some, poses a possible answer to the question before it.* To pursue the example about your unresponsive friend Samantha: you quickly (in fact, virtually at lightning speed, you come so well equipped to perform these operations) recall that people tend not to respond unless they know they are being addressed, and you say to yourself, "Maybe she didn't hear me."

3. *The mind takes that first possible answer and tests it.* Did Samantha *look* as if she hadn't heard?
4. *If the mind's first answer fills the bill, inquiry ends.* Samantha may never have made eye contact with you. She may have seemed distracted, as if she had some pressing business to see to. In addition, you may now recall her telling you yesterday that she would be going to a job interview at about this time today. That would settle that: she *hadn't* heard.

   If, however, the mind's initial hypothesis fails to survive this test—or if it survives, but other plausible hypotheses have yet to be tested—the mind plunges on. Admit it: Samantha's neglect of your greeting may have been deliberate; she seemed to face away from you at just that tilt and angle life has taught you to associate with disdain or hurt feelings. You must think harder.
5. *The mind poses and tests alternative possible answers.* Could Samantha have taken offense at some action of yours? Maybe she is aggrieved that you disputed her point about Manifest Destiny in class yesterday.
6. *When the mind cannot come up with answers that satisfy it based on facts it already possesses, it devises ways to gather additional facts.* Assuming you expect to see Samantha later in the week, you may decide to note how she greets you then.

It is not tenable, it seems to me, to maintain that only some of our students have minds capable of true inquiry when virtually all must inquire innumerable times between getting up in the morning and going to bed at night. As David Perkins observes, "Discovery depends not on special processes but on special purposes. Creating occurs when ordinary mental processes in an able person are marshaled by creative or appropriately 'unreasonable' intentions" (1981, 101).

The foremost challenge facing us teachers of writing is, I believe, not so much to *sharpen* students' thinking skills as it is to let our students know—and to demonstrate conclusively to them—that, for higher-order thinking, they already largely "have what it takes."

One good strategy for that campaign is, whenever possible, to *catch* a student in the act of thinking.

Teaching Idea 1: Sizing You Up

Your assigned lot of students arrives at your assigned classroom and dutifully fills most of the available seats. In the moments before class begins, your new students privately observe and note:

- your sex,
- your age,
- the lines on your face,
- what you're wearing,
- whether you're sitting or standing,
- what, if anything, you've written on the blackboard,
- what, if any, small talk you make until things get rolling,
- and a great deal more.

Nor, of course, do they merely "take in" these details; they *process* them. They use them as data in their pursuit of the answers to certain questions on their minds, such as, "How will I like this class, if I remain in it?" and "How will I do in this class?" If they have heard the scuttlebutt about you—and/or looked over the tables of contents in books that you require—then they juxtapose the impressions of you and your course obtained already and those being made on the spot. In any case, they are busily hypothesizing, testing their hypotheses, and *re*hypothesizing. (Nor, it goes without saying, will they cease and desist from this activity once your course gets under way.)

Exploit the situation:

- Prior to distributing a syllabus, *ask* your new students what they suspect your course will be like. Have them write out their respective hunches individually, and then open the floor to them to speak.
- Regardless what hunch a student puts forward, ask him or her (a) where that hunch came from and (b) whether *all* the facts at hand would support it.
- When the time is right, let your students know that they have thus already proven themselves capable of realizing some of your chief aims for them: they can obviously frame questions, generate and test possible answers, and live with uncertainty!

Teaching Idea 2: Eavesdropping—and Other Everyday, Familiar Forms of Inquiry

For some perverse reason, no everyday stimulus more consistently sets our wheels of inquiry turning than someone else's private business half-exposed to us. A compelling way to demonstrate to students that open-ended thinking comes naturally is to present them with the transcript of a real "half-dialogue" of someone at a public telephone, where the eavesdropper's first surmise concerning what is going on must give way to other, better understandings as more is said. (Either use one of the two partial transcripts below or plant yourself by a public phone somewhere and obtain one of your own to use.)

1. Briefly give the setting.
2. Read the transcript *in segments of no more than two or three lines at a time.*
3. At the end of each segment, simply say, "Thoughts?"
4. As students offer notions of what's happening, acknowledge these respectfully and name details that would seem to make such readings plausible.
5. Just as in Sizing You Up (above), when the trial-and-error nature of the process is sufficiently manifest, congratulate your students. Tell the lot of them that they are natural inquirers, and break the act of inquiry into its parts to bring the point home. (Don't omit to say conclusively that they came up with their own questions, which were: "What is the relationship of one speaker to the other?" and "What's going on in the lives of the two people speaking, forming the context of their talk?" You, for your part, simply said, "Thoughts?")

Two Half-Dialogues

1. Near a gate at the Atlanta Airport, a man in his thirties wearing a business suit has just placed a call.

Hi, baby.
Oh yeah?

No. I'll be home soon, though.

Is your mother there?
She what?
Is she still at the game?
Go get your mother for me. Get your mother.

Hi there. I'm in Atlanta.
Well, you know, my session got out late and there was nothing direct.

How was the game?
Ohhh, that's too bad.

Who were we playing?

When did David come *in*?
Gave up some runs?
Huh. Is he sleeping?

2. In a corridor of the student center at Bentley College, a woman in her thirties wearing a dress suit has just placed a call at a public telephone.

Hello, may I speak with Mr. Foster please? Mr. Foster, this is Janet Johnson. I have a message that you called. What can I help you with?
Uh-huh. Yes. Hmm.

No, you cannot.

I don't think that that's a good excuse, not really. I expect my midterms to be taken more seriously than that.

No. You will get an F.

No, that is out of the question too.

Really?!

▶

> I think you'll find the Dean will see things as I do, but if you feel it's necessary, don't let me stop you.
>
> Will you be in class today?
> Fine. Good-bye.

Once the point (about the naturalness of inquiry) is made, make it yet again. Much that follows in this book is *premised* on your students' recognition of themselves as thinkers.

List a few of the numerous subjects of inquiry in everyday life:

- what implications the weather forecast has for an event planned for later in the day,
- why a saved computer file cannot be retrieved,
- how to get a large piece of furniture through a doorway,
- whom to vote for,
- how to let a certain person know that one has a romantic interest in him or her.

Most of these examples—and most of the examples on pages 3–4 above—will ring bells for students generally. In addition, when you know your students well enough, you can add examples targeted to them as individuals. Well conceived, these ring *louder* bells. The student whose big sister's wedding is approaching will perk up at your suggestion that preparing invitation lists is inquiry. (The question "Whom should we invite?" generates numerous possible names, and these, in turn, are put through difficult tests.) The student who enjoys repairing cars will readily perceive how diagnosing automotive problems fits the model of good inquiry used here.

Teaching Idea 3: Difficult Riddles

When I began my teaching career, my father had but one pedagogical suggestion for me: Open every meeting of a class with a riddle—both to sharpen students' minds and to make students more attentive to whatever lesson you have planned for the day, when you get to that.

While I have yet to go that far, I do value the ability of good riddles to intrigue and to "set the wheels turning," and I typically employ them on two or three occasions in a course.

But please note: *As a teacher, my interest in riddles has nothing to do with right answers; it has only to do with full, extensive use of the mind.* "What did you do first with your mind when I put this problem to you?" "What did you do then?" "After that, what did you do?" These are the questions on which I place emphasis after students' five or ten allotted minutes to "solve" a riddle have elapsed—not, "What is the answer to this riddle?"

Sometimes, in fact, I purposely neglect to ask for the solution at all and, instead, let class members cry out for it at last. That sure turn of events sets me up to make two points I dearly wish to make with students:

1. Inquiry on difficult questions—including the majority of questions posed by college faculty in their assignments of papers—does not often yield simple, definite answers in the time available to work on them. (In that way, of course, they correspond to hard riddles posed with unreasonable time constraints.) Some such questions—for example, "What is time?" and "Do human beings possess free will?"—have remained unanswered, in the definitive sense, for thousands of years.
2. Most teachers at the college level (admittedly not all, but, in my experience, most) value full engagement of the mind *over* presentation of final, definite solutions or answers.

From this stance, I am able to validate a great many "moves of the mind" made by students. No matter that most of them lead down blind alleys—they are often just as worthy of praise as those that (it develops) lead down clear, broad avenues.

A Favorite Riddle of Mine

Question: What's going on here?

> "Time flies."
> "We cannot. Their flight is too erratic."

Answer: One person is directing another to take out a watch (or other timing device) and determine the speed of those ubiquitous insects, flies! The other person protests.

Things to Hear Students Doing

Good mental moves that students are likely to make—*and that call for recognition regardless of whether the correct solution is discovered*—include:

- hypothesizing that "Time flies" is merely a restatement of the well-known cliché;
- noting that, if the cliché hypothesis is maintained, the plural possessive "their" is nonsensical, since it has no referent within the text;
- and wondering if it is significant that (judging from the two sets of closed quotes) two speakers are involved.

For other good riddles, you could, of course, find a good book of them—or have students tell you *their* favorites.

Teaching Idea 4: Maker of the Rules

This is my version of a game I learned many years ago from two graduate students of chemistry, Charlie and Judy Lerman. Although I have scrapped their name for it, "Playing God," to spare the sensibilities of some of my students, it is still to me essentially what it was to Charlie and Judy: the play enactment of scientific inquiry, where the actual "rules of the game"—laws of the universe, if you will—are known with certainty only by their creator, and the "players" must proceed in ignorance, finding and clinging to what seems to work.

1. You (the teacher) are the Maker of the Rules. Two or more students are the players.
2. To each player, deal ten playing cards with numbers on them. Explain that the object of the game is to *get rid of all ten cards before any other player does so.*

3. Set up this simple chart on the blackboard or wall:

   Will Work

   ____
   ____
   ____
   ____
   ____

4. Privately decide the rule for determining what cards "will work"—for example, "Odd numbers alternate with even numbers." (Until students become used to the game, rules should be as simple as that.) Write the rule down, but divulge it to no one until the round is over.
5. Have the players take turns holding up a card and saying either "This *will* work" or "This *won't* work." When they are right—for example, when, by your unspoken rule, only an even-numbered card would "work" as the next card in the game, and they either hold up an even-numbered card and say "This *will* work" or hold up an odd-numbered card and say "This *won't* work"—take that card from them; they have succeeded in getting rid of it. When, however, they are wrong about the card that they hold up, have them keep it; they have not succeeded in getting rid of it.
6. As play establishes that certain cards *will* "work," add them (in exact order) to your simple "Will Work" chart, which thus becomes a growing body of data for the players to contemplate.
7. Throughout play, have the players and onlookers alike privately *write down* what the rules seem to them to be, changing their minds as often as they wish.
8. Even in the post-game review, do not rush to divulge your operative rule. Get the players to tell you what hypotheses formed the basis of their decisions, as well as their reasons for replacing initial hypotheses with new ones. Then turn to nonplayers (Monday morning quarterbacks, they) for *their* hypotheses.

Follow-Up

Tell your students of the Lermans' original name for the game. Ask them what they think of it.

Teaching Idea 5: The Reflective Journal

Of course, a great many teachers introduce students to the heuristic (and therapeutic) functions of writing by having them keep journals.

On the one hand, I have known students to keep assigned journals dutifully but with no personal interest or engagement, and, on the other hand, I have known students to become addicted to their journals, and to do much of their best thinking in them. From Day One, students being asked to keep journals need to understand the difference between journals and diaries. They need to hear that in journals people do more than simply note experiences down in order to memorialize them. In this regard, it helps, I think, to call journals "reflective journals."

Also, it helps to integrate the introduction of journals with the larger, ongoing discussion of inquiry. What, after all, are the facts and vignettes recorded in a journal but situations that raise questions? What are the speculations noted in a journal but hypotheses? And what are the bouts of reasoning transcribed there but tests of hypotheses?

It helps, as well, to provide students with diverse samples of true journal entries.

Once Journal Keeping Gets Under Way

To be sure that students *are* using their journals reflectively (i.e., inquiringly), ask them at intervals to show you representative pages. (These pages should be few in number, so that [a] no student feels obliged to disclose material that he or she deems too private and [b] you don't end up adding whole journals to your stack of papers to read.)

When students (individually or collectively) seem not to have caught on to the spirit of reflective journal keeping, consider giving them some "openers" from which to choose in writing their next entries. Creating whole sentences beginning with words and phrases like the ones below almost necessitates a shifting of the mind into reflective gear:

Ironically . . .

Of all the stories in the news this week . . .
A certain scene I witnessed today made me think of . . .
I wonder if . . .

Or pose *challenges* to students, like:

Don't stop writing till the thing you are describing—whether an intimate relationship or a section of your physics textbook—raises a question of genuine difficulty.

. . . or . . .

In writing your next entry, do not stop until some new, surprising *connection* occurs to you.

A Variant: The Dedicated Journal

In courses involving big culminating papers (see the section headed "The *Big* Paper" on pages 42–44)—as well as in courses focused on a single theme or issue throughout—have students keep a short- or long-term journal dedicated just to one crucial, relevant question or cluster of questions.

Teaching Idea 6: A Flow Chart of Inquiry

I have known many students whose understanding of inquiry improved when I went beyond concept and practice to render it visually for them. Figure 1 shows my Flow Chart of Inquiry, the latest and best-received visual I have come up with. For a full explanation of the chart, see pages 2–4 above. *Q* stands for *question, H* for *hypothesis* (or *hunch*), *T w/ F* for *testing with facts,* and *Th* for *thesis.* The large, two-headed arrow indicates that the process of hypothesizing and testing is recursive, and the many *small* arrows serve as reminders that even the best of human inquiries involve times of confusion or diversion.

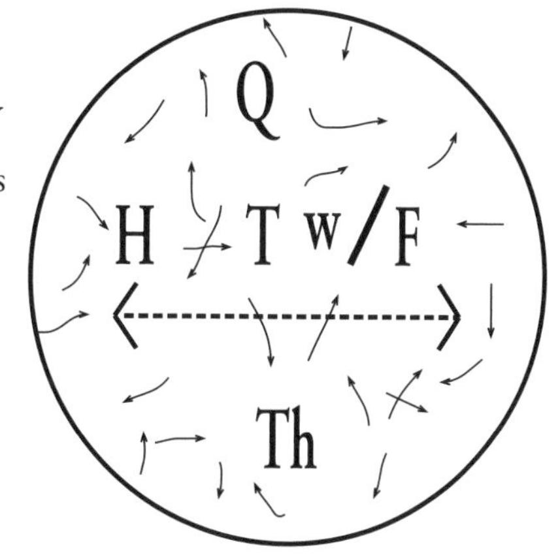

Figure 1: A flow chart of inquiry

A Note to the Reader Who Feels That This Chart Spells Out Too Much—As Well As to the Reader Who Feels That It Spells Out Too Little

I share one misgiving with one of you two readers, and another with the other. With my colleague who would say that I have gone too far here, I, too, fear the mechanistic, the "steps" that bypass what is natural and elicit the robotic. However, merely to tell students to "think"—*without* breaking thinking into steps—leaves them blank-eyed. Even though, if I shout "Think!" I am referring (as I've said) to an activity that comes quite naturally to them, they do not *see* that that is what I mean by *think*.

With my colleagues who would say that I have not gone far enough, I, too, am mindful that, in fact, each of my few "moves" here—questioning, hypothesizing, testing—subsumes a hundred smaller moves. But getting into those more numerous *sub*-operations does, it seems to me, call forth the mechanistic, the robotic.

I have aimed for what you might well call "a midrange heuristic"—a scheme sufficiently spelled out to help my students see what natural operations are intended, but not so spelled out as to distract them or to trip them up once those very operations have come into play. "Look two ways before crossing" is a midrange heuristic; the direction it provides is more specific than that given by "Be careful on the street" but less specific than that given by "Do not cross if cars approach within a hundred yards at fifty miles per hour, or within fifty yards at thirty miles per hour, or within twenty yards at fifteen miles per hour."

Likewise, "Do unto others as you would have them do unto you" is a midrange heuristic—more specific than the injunction to "act justly," but far less specific than books of law.

▶

I see "Question, hypothesize, and test" as a heuristic that falls into the same category, and my students attest to its usefulness. Once it has done its main work—namely, to activate (or to revive) the process of inquiry that comes quite naturally to us in many settings—it can be dropped altogether.

Teaching Ideas 7–13: In-Class "Think Tanks"— Supervised Practice in College-Level Inquiry

> The student needs the experience of moving into the thick of a phenomenon and discovering the difficulties that accompany any responsible attempt to account for it. . . . The aim . . . is not . . . to come up with a neat causal explanation for the event but to gain a respect for its complexity, to develop a taste for facts and information and a tolerance for answers that apply in some contexts but not in others or that point up the need for new questions.
>
> —Mina P. Shaughnessy, *Errors and Expectations* (1977, 265)

Once your students are familiar with your *model* of inquiry (whether it's the same model introduced above or a model of your own), they will be curious to know *what such work of the mind sounds like when applied to questions asked at school.* You can most effectively convey the "sound"—or "feel"—of academic inquiry to them by having them do some in class, with you for coach. If their in-class attempts at it go well, they will be forcibly impressed by how natural a process it is, by how similar in "sound" and "feel" it is to everyday inquiry on personal questions, and by how well equipped they are to do it.

Teaching Idea 7: The Initial Think Tank

For a first case, use a question on which there is available a train of thought that you consider exemplary: one incorporating all the basic moves of inquiry included in your model, but doing so in the familiar, unintimidating voice of a student.

The question I myself use is: "Interpret William Carlos Williams's poem 'The Red Wheelbarrow.'" The train of thought I use (written by me, in the voice of a student) opens as follows:

The Red Wheelbarrow

so much depends
upon

a red wheel
barrow

glazed with rain
water

beside the white
chickens.

What does William Carlos Williams try to say in his "The Red Wheelbarrow"?
Nothing, if you ask me.
It's just a description, a nice picture—
wheelbarrow, just after a rain,
there's no one around
(did the people living there take shelter from this rain?
is *that* why they're nowhere in sight?)
no, no one living but some white chickens.
Actually, the more I think of it,
the nicer, more pleasing, this picture becomes.
And isn't that enough—
to please a reader by description? A writer doesn't always
have to be "saying" something.

Let me look at the poem again, in case I missed something my first time through.
"So much depends"
"depends"—
What the hell am I supposed to do with "depends"?
"depends upon" = can't do without. Right?
What can't do without that wheelbarrow?

For the complete text, suitable to download and copy for students, please see my Web site at http://www.ncte.org/books/59133/resources/. (The complete text appears there twice—the second time, annotated to point out intellectual moves being made within it.)

1. With whatever question you've selected for the purpose, have your students "think on paper" as they try to answer it—rather than think and *then* write. That is, have them transcribe their thinking as they are doing it, in all of its inherent messiness. (This might be the right time for providing Background Music; see page 27.)
2. After five or ten minutes—or as soon as class members seem to be running out of pertinent ideas—interrupt them and call on some of them to share what thoughts they've had.
3. Having thus pulled off a "cross-infusion" of new thoughts among class members, invite one and all to resume their respective private trains of thought.
4. When four or five additional minutes have passed, bring an end to thinking and transcribing, and refer all eyes to your preselected *strong* train of thought. Find out . . .

- how your students would rate it as a specimen of inquiry
- and whether it compares favorably or unfavorably with their own trains of thought.

Be prepared to hear some students assign low marks to the very sort of thinking to which you've hoped they would aspire, simply because the thinker's real-time record of it is informal and disorganized. Be prepared to defend your selection of the transcript (unless, of course, your students manage to convince you of deficiencies in it as inquiry).

Also, if you feel as I do about inquiry, be prepared to say, "Not only don't I mind the messiness of that train of thought, I am skeptical when, in response to a question of true difficulty, someone's first thoughts are *not* messy. Thinking at its best is messy."

And be prepared to say, "Rest assured, good organization, clarity, and even maturity of style will have their ample day in this course—but not until later, when we take up the needs and expectations of one's readers."

Do Trains of Thought Need to Be Written Down?

Certainly, people differ as to how much the process of writing thoughts down furthers their thinking. For millions of people, including myself, writing thoughts down *accelerates* the course of inquiry's normal trial and error, and it does so quite simply by putting all errors onto a surface outside the mind, where one can get a good look at them.

I can still remember when this great advantage to writing things down came home to me. I was only thirty or forty minutes into a train of thought on a vexing problem, and already I had run through and eliminated several possible solutions. I then wrote, "I'm getting nowhere fast." Fortunately, even in my frustration I saw that I had inadvertently put my finger on one of the powers of writing; I realized that my several possible solutions had been *destined* to reveal their flaws to me sooner or later, and that writing those solutions out had surfaced their flaws rapidly, saving me most of my available thinking time for other, more promising alternatives. All hard inquiry involves a stretch of time (sometimes several stretches) of getting nowhere, but with writing's help one can get to nowhere fast and then make progress. ▶

In addition, writing one's thoughts down creates a *written record*, on which one can draw extensively in producing the paper, memorandum, or book expected by others. One's ultimate reader will want to know: what solutions were rejected and why; what facts were used in testing the solution endorsed; and so on.

Needless to say, written records of one's thought can take forms quite unlike the transcript found on pages 16–17 of this book. Some people prefer "maps" of thought, in which ideas and facts are set down in clusters or connected by arrows to show the relationships between them. Others are (like myself) devotees of the three-by-five index card; they give each thought or fact its own small card upon arrival, and so *put off* organizing things.

And, of course, one can do virtually all of the above on a computer, if one chooses to.

Except when—as in many writing courses—teachers *read* one's thought-notes and expect to understand them, they can be mere sentence fragments, rather than whole sentences. In general, of course, only the writer needs to be able to understand them.

Teaching Idea 8: Subsequent Think Tanks

Your students will have what it takes to do the mind's work you ask of them, but many will mightily resist you at first. They will proceed as they always have. When you request a train of thought, they'll submit a simple essay-like paragraph or two, more or less subordinated to a single, predetermined take on the question posed. If you, dismayed, refer them to your model train of thought (see Teaching Idea 7) to impress upon them how profoundly different that is from the work they have submitted, some may well still give you an essay the next time, but with line breaks!

An effective teacher emulates the sun. There is no surer way to get a "thaw" going than to keep the heat turned on.

Do not stop at one train of thought; repeatedly give your students good, intensive *practice* in inquiry. Present them with intriguing source materials. (Examples of such source materials, which I call "grist," appear below.) In the time you set aside in class for students to think, have them go as far toward answering a question on that source material as they can get, without distorting or unduly simplifying. Let them make as few or as many notes as they like while they think, and let them write their notes either as full sentences or as single words and phrases.

Let them write their notes directly on the source materials, on separate sheets of paper, on self-stick notes, on index cards. (The latter two items may need to be brought in by you. And you may also want to make available certain writing *implements* that students will not have with them, such as highlighting markers.) *Encourage every student to proceed in the way that best suits him or her.*

Grist for the Early Think Tanks

Various items qualify as intriguing academic source materials for early Think Tanks:

Elusive Poems and Short Stories

By "elusive" I mean resistant to quick or easy explication. In every good school or public library can be found hundreds of works that qualify.

When I frame questions about such works—unless I am teaching a course in literature—I avoid the jargon of literary criticism in class. I ask, "What is this poet (or author) 'saying' to the reader?" For example:

> Half the world or more seems to believe that Robert Frost's "The Road Not Taken" is a call to the young to blaze new paths. Are we, however, meant to *accept* the speaker's claim that he "took the [road] less traveled by"? And if a close reading of the poem would suggest that we are *not* meant to accept that claim, what *is* the poet's stance, vis-à-vis his speaker? (My colleague Robert Sprich has convinced me to pay serious attention to the possibility that in the last stanza—beginning with the words "I shall be telling this with a sigh"—the speaker inadvertently reveals a tendency to simplify his past and glorify himself!)

Short stories that stand out for similarly rich ambiguity include Sherwood Anderson's "The Egg" and Luisa Valenzuela's "Tango."

Works of Art

Here, for example, is a painting by Emily Hiestand (see Figure 2). What is it supposed to convey? Do students' answers to that question take into account all of the work's elements? How would it affect them to know that Hiestand titled her painting "Tea Party with Bomber"—or that she painted it in 1983?

Figure 2: Painting by Emily Hiestand

Charts and Graphs

What a teacher needs is not just any chart or graph, but a chart or graph that both raises questions and contains data sufficient (in complexity, as well as in quantity) to *fuel sustained consideration of those questions.*

For example, in 1997 a Gallup poll asked residents of sixteen countries, "For you personally, do you think it is necessary or not necessary to have a child at some point in your life in order to feel fulfilled?" One might have one's students read the results and try to determine why responses of "Yes" to the question ranged from a low of 46 percent to a high of 94 percent. When I did that with a class of mine, students first took note of the fact that the low (46 percent) response was that of Americans, and they hypothesized that responses corresponded to levels of national prosperity. However, that hypothesis seemed to hold for *certain* countries—India at 93 percent, Thailand at 85 percent—but not for *all* countries—not for Taiwan at 87 percent or France at 73 percent.

Students' other hypotheses also ran into problems. If religious attitudes on birth control were crucial, how could one account for the fact that predominantly Catholic countries like Spain, Mexico, and Colombia produced results closer to those of the United States than to those at the other end?

In addition, some students raised excellent methodological concerns: Was the male/female breakdown of respondents the same in each country? Was the age breakdown the same? What, exactly, *were* the male/female and age breakdowns?

For some suitable charts and graphs in the public domain, see my Web site at http://www.ncte.org/books/59133/resources/, from which you are welcome to download them.

Sundry Difficult Questions

Since the only thing provided to students in this case is questions—and since, in Think Tanks, no opportunity exists to visit one's library—the questions must be ones on which students are likely to have relevant ideas and facts in memory. Among such questions, I would include:

> Arm on the left, arm on the right. Eye on the left, eye on the right. Nose in the middle. Mouth in the middle.—Why is the human body so symmetrical?
>
> What, exactly, *is* it about good jokes that makes people laugh?
>
> How, if at all, does a person's way of deciding between right and wrong change from the age of two to your age?

Again, these and other usable questions can be found on my Web site. (As with all of the Web site materials listed in this book, help yourself.)

Although the inquiries these questions set in motion would all *benefit* from some research, they can be sustained—initially at least—for long periods of time without it. Indeed, a Think Tank challenge of this sort enables us to feature memory as an essential resource in thought. Far too often, students rule germane firsthand and secondhand experience out of order and confine themselves to the published works of putative experts. (In the margin of one student's psychology paper on dreams, I once saw a teacher's comment saying, in effect, "You write like someone who, in all her years of daily sleep, has never had a dream herself.")

Grist for the Later Think Tanks

The particular materials I recommend above are primary sources and raw data. At a certain point in your course, however, students would benefit from in-class Think Tank sessions involving secondary sources as well, since most of the research assigned by their other instructors will include secondary sources. You might choose to proceed as I have:

1. Identify two or three questions of interest.
2. For each such question assemble a small *set* of source materials. . .

   - at least one of which has *no or little relevance* to the question (just as most books that students will find online or at their fingertips in libraries have no or little relevance to their respective questions);
   - at least one of which contains passages that most class members *will not understand well*, unless they reread them and/or consult a dictionary;
   - at least one of which takes a position *clearly opposed* to that taken by another source;
   - at least one of which takes a *complicated, qualified, or speculative* position;
   - at least one of which *lacks hard evidence* for claims;
   - and at least one of which *raises questions of validity for other reasons,* such as date of publication (in subject areas where

research produces new knowledge at a fast pace) or author's bias.

Although half a dozen specifications are listed here, try to satisfy them all with three or, at the most, four short pieces or excerpts. Recall how short your class time is.

Interviews

After each spell of thinking in a Think Tank, conduct an in-class exchange with one or two students likely to have done passably well at the challenge. Have them return in their minds to the moment when you posed your question to them, turning them loose, and ask them to recount all that they can still remember having thought on the question, in the order that they thought it. (Some or much of what they have to recount may be reflected in notes that they've taken. If so, encourage them to refer to such notes as they speak.)

Then, ask them to listen closely to you as you state your understanding of their accounts, to be able to correct your understanding or to add to it. As you proceed, use terms drawn from your *model* of inquiry. Where, for example, a student says, "But when I looked at the numbers for 1993, they didn't support my theory," a teacher might say, "On testing your hypothesis with facts—namely, the facts for 1993—you discovered . . ."

Having let the student make corrections or additions to your version of his or her story of inquiry, wax even bolder and presume to name the respects in which the inquiry recounted was strong and those in which it was weak, again using terms from your model, as in the in-class teacher comments below:

> I was struck by the pains you took to clarify terms in the original question. Yes, "improved" is a vague word; you were wise to stipulate what it would mean when *you* used it. That way, you gave precision to your thinking.
>
> Your first hypothesis was a predictable one—echoing the popular talk shows these days—but still definitely one worth considering. . . .
>
> My reservations about this inquiry are twofold: first, as soon as you hit upon a possible answer—a hypothesis—that fit just one of the available facts, you settled for that

answer, didn't bother with facts farther down your chart, which might have proven inconvenient.

Secondly . . .

Every such evaluation should, I feel, give the last word to the student him- or herself. Ask the student, "Is that how *you* would assess the thinking that you did?" Then, as appropriate, agree to disagree—but don't be disagreeable. *Be respectful.* If and when I undermine a student's faith in his or her capacity to judge matters, I remove the basis on which all else rests. One can disagree—and be heard as disagreeing—without damaging a student's self-esteem as thinker. (For more along these lines, see the following section.)

Teaching Idea 9: Pulling for More—By Honoring a Student's Thinking

The human mind's work, since it never can escape the strictures of trial and error, is, in transcript form, a terrible recursive muddle. What is more, the mind's *best* work tends, if anything, to be messier than normal. But students do not generally know these things. In the public world of well-organized, coherent "experts"—who always put their necessary messes behind them before they take to print or podium—students are liable to view the welter of questions, impressions, and contradictions filling their own minds as proof of their inadequacy.

Nor have most of them already had teachers who strive to counteract their misunderstanding of their own minds. On the contrary.

During four terms on my local school board, I sat in and observed more than 120 classes at the elementary and secondary levels, and I must report that many teachers do precisely as some critics charge: they reward only "right answers"—not good inquiry that does not, in the time allotted, produce right answers, but only right answers, regardless of how they are obtained. There are still math teachers (not all math teachers, fortunately, but many) who open class by asking their students to "call out the answers" on the previous night's homework and who respond to each wrong answer with that devastating one-word comment, "Class?" There are still history teachers who assign study questions at the ends of chapters and give credit on interpretive matters (like, "What were the real causes of the Civil War?") only for those answers that blithely, uncritically paraphrase the published text.

Once a student's thinking is exposed to view and we can discuss it, we need, I feel, to counteract such well-intentioned, ill-advised teaching. We need to *honor* the student as a thinker—to affirm her membership in the same species that includes all the experts.

The student needs to know that discovering contradictory evidence is not a sign that his mind was deficient in coming up with its initial, flawed hypothesis, but, in fact, a sign that his mind is working well indeed. The student needs to know much the same about discovering ambiguity in the question at hand, about discovering gaps in his knowledge which need filling before he can make further progress, and so on.

Although this honoring might well take an explicit form, as in the first of my three teacher comments above (page 24), it can be effected just as well, or better, by implicit means, such as an uncritical *engagement* with the student's thoughts. William Perry used to tell of a teacher of his who, in their periodic conferences, inspired Bill to take a certain project further and further just by sitting attentively across his desk from Bill and going, "Uh-huh, uh-huh." Of course, he might have used words that conveyed more than "uh-huh" and still struck a perfectly uncritical note. He might have said, "Huh. Never looked at the question that way before," or, "Now I think I see how this thinking goes back to the insight that you had last week about astrology." The effect on motivation should hardly surprise us. Is there any response more reinforcing than another's interest?

The pedagogical paradox here has not entirely escaped me, but I leave it to Peter Elbow to state:

> When I had a teacher who believed in me, who was interested in me and interested in what I had to say, I wrote well. When I had a teacher who thought I was naive, dumb, silly, and in need of being "straightened out," I wrote badly and sometimes couldn't write at all. Here is an interestingly paradoxical instance of the social-to-private principle from Vygotsky and Meade: we learn to listen better and more trustingly to *ourselves* through interaction with trusting *others*. (1987, 65)

Teaching Idea 10: Pulling for More—By Using Tuneless Background Music

On one or two of the occasions in a course when I set my students the task of "thinking on paper" about a certain question during class time (see pages 15–24), I myself meanwhile quietly intone a list of exhortations to them designed to induce the state of mind required for unconstrained inquiry. My script:

> Be sure that you're writing for yourself now, not for an audience. This is you speaking to you, thinking on paper.
>
> As a hunch—a possible answer to your question—occurs to you, put it down, play it out . . . then, test it.
>
> Keep it honest. Don't stick to some hunch that does not truly survive your testing. Try out *other* possible answers.
>
> Bring *all* your resources to bear: firsthand experience, secondhand experience, reasoning, intuition, etc.
>
> *Leave room for uncertainty.*
>
> Think about what gaps in your knowledge you may need to fill to be able to answer your question with *more* certainty—and about how you might fill those gaps.

Some students find these coaching sounds intrusive as they try to think and write. With their needs in mind, I speak softly and limit the number of times I read the list out loud in class (two times through, per day used). Also, before starting, I direct my students to ignore me, to "tune me out," whenever they feel that they are going strong, making good progress without my help.

In the end, more students voice appreciation for my unstrung music than object to it. A few go so far as to request encores.

When it works, this "background music"—a variant of coaching from the sidelines—actually stops many students in their customary tracks and sends them down new paths. They are, perhaps, "experiential learners." My prefatory, conceptual remarks about inquiry may benefit them little.

When it works well indeed, this "music" is internalized by students; they hear it ringing in their ears when difficult (academic or nonacademic) questions confront them in the future.

Teaching Idea 11: Pushing for More—By Playing Devil's Advocate

I have paired the two preceding teaching ideas as "Pulling for More" because they both require of a teacher the stance of a coach or personal advocate. That is, they involve telling—or implicitly telling—a student that he or she "has what it takes" to think more fully, more extensively. Arguably, though, just as effective a stance—*more* effective for certain students—is the agonistic one, the stance of opposition: "*pushing* for more."

Occasionally, play the role of devil's advocate with your students. Better yet, get your students to play devil's advocate with each other. Play the role yourself initially, to give your students all the perverse inspiration it requires, and then, when you observe that they have caught the (mean) spirit of the thing, let them go and do likewise, classmate unto classmate.

They should . . .

- *Show no mercy.* Any praise—even faint praise, like "You make some good points, Alice, but . . ."—compromises the intended spirit of the exercise. The only way to ensure that no student feels put down is to allow *nothing but* criticism to be uttered. (Let Alice tell herself, "*Of course* the devil's advocate had nothing nice to say about my thinking: playing nice is not allowed!")
- *Look for every sort of error in thinking which it is possible to commit,* including:
  - misreading the question,
  - having thoughts irrelevant to the question,
  - failing to *test* one's answer to the question,
  - failing to identify and deal with *alternative* answers,
  - failing to acknowledge complexity,
  - making false assumptions,
  - and reasoning poorly in other ways.

How Much Thinking Is Enough?

Mina Shaughnessy has framed the problem well:

> One writer may take a volume or more to make his case among his peers while another leaps within

> the limits of a personal essay from an account of his experience to a generalization that embraces mankind—and both may gain acceptance from their peers. Thus Piaget will attempt to describe the world as children perceive it by drawing extensively upon laboratory observations to support his point. But Orwell will use in one essay his own recollected experience as a student at an English boarding school to generalize about children's perceptions of the adult world. Each writer has set for himself a different task, different in scope and in kind of analysis. In doing so he has had in mind his own resources as a thinker and writer, the nature of his data, the demands of the marketplace, and the realities of his work schedule. (1977, 270–71)

All that needs adding to Shaughnessy's practical wisdom here is the sobering recognition that—for making *absolutely* certain of a claim—*nothing* is enough. As John Locke, David Hume, and others understood some centuries ago, any day may bring into our hands a datum that will overturn the surest, most "self-evident" of human truths. As powerful as reason is, it never does attain answers "beyond all doubt." (Ask Newton or his latter-day supplanter, Einstein.) Inquiry into a matter can always be revived.

Somehow we manage to live with this knowledge. It keeps us—well, if not humble, tolerant at least, or even open-minded.

In the end then, on the question "How much thinking is enough?", I have settled for saying the foregoing and, like Shaughnessy, for giving students guidance in the form of diverse models to consider.

Teaching Idea 12: A Field Trip to the Library (The *Larger* World of "Grist")

Of course, students who are unfamiliar with the library—and with basics of library use—lack genuine access to most of the most valuable resource materials on campus. In addition, it could be argued, their unfamiliarity often deepens their timidity about books (see pages 35–36). They become convinced that, when it comes to words in print, they are simply "in over their heads."

Activities possible on a field trip to the library include:

- an orientation session led (or co-led) by a reference librarian…
  - about the various resources your library contains;
  - about the trial and error entailed in finding the best *heading* by which to access material on a given question;
  - about discriminating among sources on the basis of validity (by author bias, by date of publication in areas where research continues to produce significant new knowledge; and so on);
  - about reference librarians' availability!
- and just browsing:

  Set your students *loose* in the library. Challenge each of them to find a fact or an idea that is new to him or her and that piques his/her interest. At the time set for reassembling, let everyone report that "find." (The object here is plain enough: to associate the library with intellectual adventure, with the mind's play, as well as to make it more familiar territory.)

Assuming that your students now have access to the World Wide Web and other electronic resources, you or a librarian might do with *them* what I suggest above you do with libraries.

Teaching Idea 13: Group Inquiry (A Think Tank Variant)

In the real world, inquiry is rarely completely solitary. In many settings, in fact, inquiry-by-team is the prevailing modus operandi.

Once students are beginning to think more fully and extensively as individuals, they need opportunities to think together, and to ponder how private inquiry and group inquiry compare. Can the same basic moves of the mind be observed in either case? (Yes, I say.) Does each group member's contribution reflect all of the basic operations of inquiry, or does one group member tend always to offer answers to the question at hand, while another tends always to point out problems with those answers, or to ask for clarification, or to lead the group in planning what to do next?

If members' contributions do tend to differ in nature, is that problematic? What of group members who do not contribute at all? Is it problematic for them to take free rides and let others in the group do their thinking for them?

To set group inquiry in motion, you might:

- involve the whole class in *one* inquiry
- or list several possible topics of inquiry and have class members form small groups based on interests that are shared.

Use a short, stunning question, like:

> Does thought require language?

Or, use a long, elaborated question, like:

> Increasingly, health maintenance organizations (HMOs) find themselves wrestling with the moral implications of their allocation of resources. By what guideline—or guidelines—should they decide between investing in more preventative services for the young and investing in more life-prolonging technology for the old?

Once again, you are most welcome to draw possible questions for inquiry, as well as primary source materials, from my Web site: http://www.ncte.org/books/59133/resources/.

Teaching Ideas 14–20: Teaching Inquiry, Form by Form

Summary, synthesis, critique, case analysis . . . . We have, perhaps, made too much of what distinguishes one species of academic prose from another without first conveying to students that all these prose forms presuppose inquiry, as defined above. Students need to understand that all of the prose forms are, in fact, *forms used by writers to report their progress on questions.* The type of question being addressed will vary from form to form; the sorts of facts usable in testing hypotheses will vary; but the basic moves—questioning, hypothesizing, testing, rehypothesizing—will apply to all of these forms.

One may here object that summary hardly qualifies as inquiry, since a summarizer merely condenses someone else's thought and puts it into his or her own words. What does it take to accomplish that feat, however? What, if not inquiry precisely as described and drawn above (pages 2–4 and 13)?

Mike Rose inserts a telling adverbial phrase in the following sentence in *Lives on the Boundary*:

> It would give [students] a nice sense of mastery if they could determine and express the gist of readings that might, at first glance, seem opaque as medieval texts. (1990, 139)

The telling phrase is "at first glance." When we direct students to read a dialogue by Plato and to summarize it in one page, we usually neglect to mention the task's inherent difficulty. What is more, through this neglect of ours, we let many students persist in their false notion that a truly competent member of the class would comprehend the text just in ingesting it "at first glance."

Whether consciously or not, we practice inquiry even "just" to penetrate challenging texts.

- We apply a *question* to them: "What is this author trying to say to me?"
- We *hypothesize.* We pick up cues even in an author's title and in preliminary, scene-setting passages to form a tentative sense of what his or her point is likely to be.
- We *test.* As further statements by the author come our way, we hold them up against our first hypothesis—that is, our initial understanding of his or her main idea—to see if they fit it.
- As we discover discrepancies, we *rehypothesize.*

Ann Berthoff has it right, I believe, when she says, "How we construe is how we construct" (1978, 6). We employ the same few mind-maneuvers to understand *another's* ideas as to produce our own. Unless the text to be summarized is simple fare indeed, it will not be fathomed "at first glance."

Teaching Idea 14: Power Summary

1. Have your class read a published piece of difficult expository prose, but one where the difficulty is purely conceptual in nature, rather than difficulty involving undefined technical terms (as in Plato's *Crito* or a *textbook* explanation of radiometric dating).
2. As individual class members finish a first read-through, have them immediately turn the text over. Then, have all members of the class take pen in hand and summarize the text from memory.
3. Next, permit them to look at the original text again.
4. Have them write a new summary now—unless the first that they wrote still satisfies them.
5. Invite students to recount their *reactions* to the experience of doing this exercise. (Indifference? Frustration? Surprise?)
6. As it develops that most class members have surprised and impressed themselves with their ability to get past initial confusion (or despair), don't be shy about claiming for summarizing the credit it deserves as a procedure of considerable power—or about naming the respects in which summarizing is like all other types of inquiry.[3]

Teaching Idea 15: Rank-Ordering Summaries

Give your students another, comparably difficult piece, along with three or four student summaries of it—at least one of which is at points inaccurate, and at least one of which omits an important idea of the author's altogether. Then, have them place the summaries in order from best to worst, and discuss.

Teaching Idea 16: From Jumbled Array to Synthesis

Just as summary starts with a question ("What is this author trying to say to me?"), so, too, does synthesis: "What relationship does Text or Thing X bear to Text or Thing Y?"

Among the sorts of hypotheses we generate when tackling the synthesizing question, these are perhaps the most common:

- X is *like* Y in some ways, *un*like Y in other ways *(comparison/contrast);*
- X is an *instance* of Y *(exemplification);*
- and X is a *cause* of Y *(cause and effect).*

Before setting students loose on pairs (or larger sets) of sources—asking them only the synthesizing question above—do as Mina Shaughnessy (1977, 246–49, 260–61) would: give them some in-class warm-ups to do. Present them with jumbled arrays of familiar and/or self-explanatory facts, and challenge them to draw from these arrays to formulate synthesizing hypotheses of all three sorts. For example, have them try this jumbled array:

dizziness	asphalt	blindfold
right-handedness	ignorance	fetus
wet paint	gymnastics	recycling
investment	midterm exams	pacifier
Inaugural Address	birthday	photographic negative
light years	metric system	verbs
the right to strike	Christopher Columbus	strawberry jam
Siberia	elephant burial ground	acupuncture
Michael Jordan	electric blender	volcano
balance of trade	index	First Lady
story	home stretch	checkmate
plutonium	envy	ambition
brilliance	table	quotation

If you challenge your students to synthesize by *comparison/contrast*, you might get sentences like:

> Midterm exams and birthdays both make the days on which they fall feel special—but birthdays tend to be more pleasant than midterm exams.

If by *exemplification:*

> Among the words and phrases in the President's Inaugural Address that annoyed me was the long-used phrase "First Lady."

If by *cause and effect:*

> If we have no need to fear being blinded by the brilliance of stars, that's because of their distance from us, which is normally measured in light years.

To Note

It is probably no favor to students, when giving them *texts* to synthesize, to choose ones that lend themselves *too neatly* to use of one of the dominant types of relationship discussed above. Rather than foster a boilerplate approach—applicable to few real-life cases—we can make of such assignments occasions to "pull for complexity." We can create pairs of texts where superficial reading would yield syntheses that closer reading would expose as simplistic.

Teaching Idea 17: The Phony Lecture and the Phony Reading

> Look out, kid. They keep it all hid.
>
> —Bob Dylan, "Subterranean Homesick Blues"

One day twelve or thirteen years ago, I was sitting in the class of a Bentley College colleague while her students read and tried to summarize an article about Sir Francis Bacon. The article portrayed Bacon as someone who on all occasions thought for himself. No matter, for example, if Aristotle had informed the world that cold water comes to a boil faster than hot water does—no matter, indeed, if Aristotle's dictum had gone unchallenged for some two millennia—Bacon would put the claim to his own test (and, by the way, prove it wrong). Plainly, the passage's main point was expressed in the author's line, "Bacon had little regard for authority."

The student whom my colleague first called upon to summarize the passage made one of the most developmentally interesting mistakes I have ever been on hand to witness. He said that the passage's gist was, "Francis Bacon didn't care about the truth."

Without my prior exposure to William Perry's work on intellectual development—and, to my good fortune, my occasional encounters with Bill Perry the man—I might well have let this breathtaking substitution of "truth" for "authority" simply pass as carelessness. With Perry in mind, however, I was—and am—inclined to see the response not as accident or error, but as probable sign of one student's personal epistemology: to him, I would venture, "authority" and "truth" were equivalent terms. That same student may have felt qualified, Bacon-like, to do his own thinking in certain domains, such as sports or fashion design, but at school, as he saw it, diverse adults (his professor, published experts, and the like) were veritable *spokespersons* for truth. His job ended with heeding and absorbing.

Which leads me to the type of paper called critique, where one's question is neither "What is this author trying to say to me?" (summary's question) nor "How does what this author is saying relate to what other authors have said?" (the synthetic question)—but "Is what this author is saying true?" Often, critique requires that a student writer consult firsthand experience; always, it requires that the student use his or her own judgment.

The Phony Lecture

In the October 1990 issue of *Life,* David Owen recounts the day when his sixth-grade teacher, Mr. Whitson, delivered a lecture to the class on the cattywampus, "an ill-adapted nocturnal animal that was wiped out during the Ice Age." Owen, along with all of his classmates, failed the quiz that followed, in which they tried to give their teacher back what he had said. The teacher's explanation was simple: "He had made up all that stuff about the cattywampus. The information in our notes and on our tests was therefore incorrect. Did we expect credit for incorrect answers? There had never been any such animal."

To create a credibility gap, the teacher had larded his lecture with contradictions and improbabilities, but that made no difference to the outcome:

> At the very moment he had been passing around the cattywampus skull (in truth, a cat's), hadn't he been telling us that no trace of the animal remained? He had described its amazing night vision, the color of its fur and any number of other facts he couldn't possibly have known. He had given the animal a ridiculous name, and we still hadn't been suspicious.

Owen credits Mr. Whitson with imbuing him and other students with a healthy skepticism that has lasted well into adulthood.

Other straight-faced hoaxes to trot out:

- patently false etymologies of common words ("man" from "manhole," "pit" from "avocado"!), or . . .
- the claim that writing has become more laborious since the inception of word processing.

The Phony Reading

Alternatively . . .

1. Give your students a passage to read in which all manner of flawed thought—irrelevance, internal contradiction, lack of evidence, inaccuracy, and so on—is purposely planted. Do not, however, identify it as such.

   One passage that qualifies is the one entitled "Mozart's Childhood" on my Web site at http://www.ncte.org/books/59133/resources/—a purposely (nay, shamelessly) doctored version of Stendahl's original, in which, for example, the opening sentence is incomprehensible gibberish and the last (framed as a conclusion) is a blatant contradiction of all that precedes it.

2. Have your students take ten minutes to write a response to the passage. (Do not stipulate what sort of response.)
3. Invite students to share their comments with the whole class.
4. Tell all.

In discussion, issues likely to be raised include:

- What assumptions does a student make on being assigned a published text to read? (What assumptions does she or he make about its value in the teacher's mind? What assumptions does she or he make about its truth value?)
- Do teachers generally *welcome* disagreement?

Teaching Idea 18: Writing in the Margin—Summary, Synthesis, and Critique Combined

Good critical reading entails keeping all three academic questions in the air at once:

- the summarizing question: "What, exactly, am I being told?"
- the synthesizing question: "How does what I'm being told relate to other things I know or have been told?"
- and the critiquing question: "Should I, in the end, *believe* what I'm being told?"

Therefore . . .

1. Give your students an article or book chapter that invites questions of all three kinds: questions of comprehension, questions of relatedness, and questions of truth value. Be sure to leave wide margins on the copies you distribute.
2. Identify a logical breaking point midway through the article or chapter, and ask your students to read up to that point, using the margins to note every critical reaction they have along the way.
3. When they have made all their marginal notes, give your students second copies of the same half-article, but with your own reactions added in the margin, as in Figure 3.

For a clean (unmarked) copy of this article—in its entirety, available to you to download—go to my Web site at http://www.ncte.org/books/59133/resources/. For the same article *with marks*, also go to my Web site.

4. Ask your students to say how their margins and yours compare. (In particular: Do as many *kinds* of reaction appear in students' margins as in yours? Which kinds do not?)

5. Repeat Steps 2, 3, and 4 for the *second* half of the article or book chapter. Do students catch on? Do they make fuller use of their margins (and minds)?

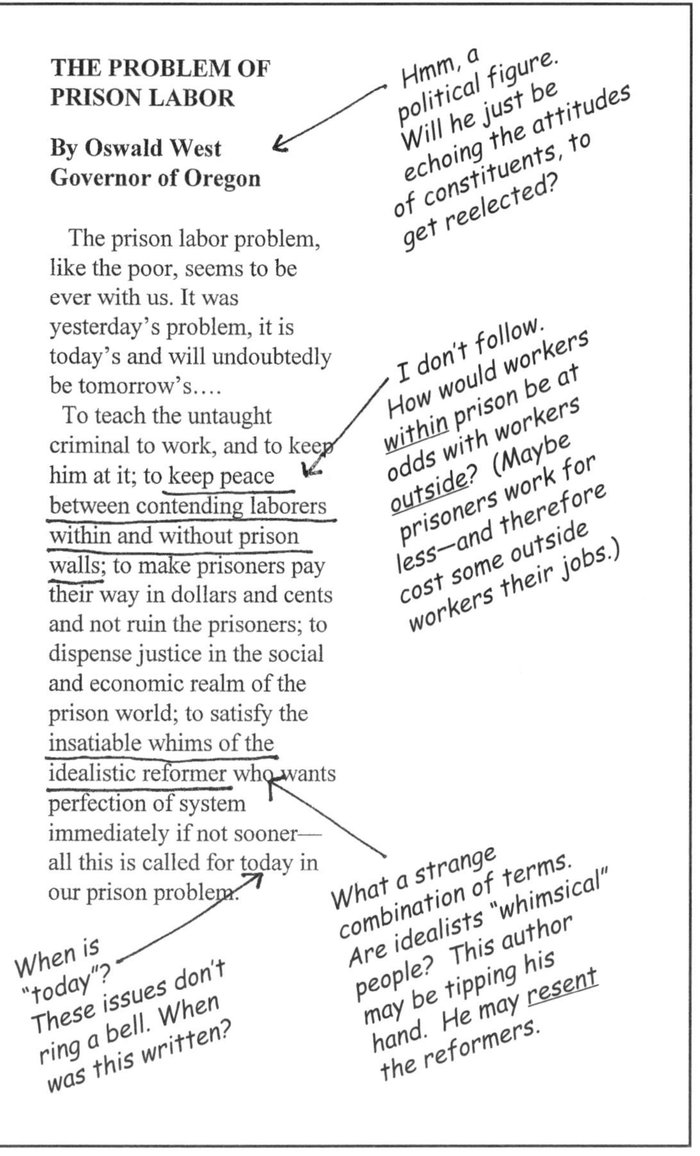

THE PROBLEM OF PRISON LABOR

By Oswald West
Governor of Oregon

The prison labor problem, like the poor, seems to be ever with us. It was yesterday's problem, it is today's and will undoubtedly be tomorrow's....

To teach the untaught criminal to work, and to keep him at it; to keep peace between contending laborers within and without prison walls; to make prisoners pay their way in dollars and cents and not ruin the prisoners; to dispense justice in the social and economic realm of the prison world; to satisfy the insatiable whims of the idealistic reformer who wants perfection of system immediately if not sooner—all this is called for today in our prison problem.

Figure 3: Partial article with teacher's marginal notes

What to Do about Assumptions

My good reader may note a certain lack of substance in this section. Sadly, nothing I have tried over the years has seemed to me to increase my students' ability to name the unspoken *premises* of arguments—an ability that (to put it mildly) comes in handy in formulating a critique.

For the record, I have tried . . .

- introducing—and promoting the use of—a single (I thought, powerful) heuristic question: "What else would have to be true if this claim were true?";
- distributing and reviewing a list of common logical fallacies, such as either/or, post hoc ergo propter hoc, and so on;
- presenting a grid of the logical categories of necessity and sufficiency—necessary and sufficient, necessary but insufficient, unnecessary but sufficient, neither necessary nor sufficient.

I urge any reader with happier results to report along these lines to contact me at: lweinstein@bentley.edu; or, The English Department, Bentley College, Waltham, MA 02452. Thank you in advance.

Teaching Idea 19: The Personal Essay

Marion Bishop, a former colleague of mine at Bentley College, once put forward a proposal to create a new course in essay writing. In that proposal, she asserted:

> Too often personal essays get put on the bottom of the essay ladder. We look at them as a stepping-stone to more complicated ways of writing. I think this perspective neglects the fact that although personal essayists' evidence comes from their own lives, these essayists still must deal with that evidence in complex, critical ways. . . . Good personal essays are not just stories with morals, they are sophisticated explorations of complicated ideas.

I agree—and might go even further than that. The good personal essay can, it seems to me, be *harder* to produce than an ambitious research paper. The personal essayist, like the researcher, starts with questions: "Why did I not go to that prom?" or "How, if at all, was I changed by my service in Vietnam?" However, many of the essayist's wrong first hypotheses prove harder for their author to catch than wrong first hypotheses in research do. The essayist's are often lines that that person has "fed" him- or herself for years—ways of explaining that cut down on pain, confusion, or social embarrassment. That is, essayists tend to be more *invested* in the false (or defective) answers which first come to them.

In addition, "conventional wisdom" plays an obstructive part. Ernest Hemingway believed his greatest challenge as a writer was "knowing what [he] really felt, rather than what [he was] supposed to feel, or had been taught to feel. . . ."

Certainly, the personal essay—rightly conceived—has little in common with dull, safe papers entitled "What I Did on My Summer Vacation." Consider having students read a sample of that dull genre, then a fine, penetrating personal essay. How do they name the differences between the two? "Obvious" and "not so obvious"? "Shallow" and "deep"? (At one point in *Hunger of Memory,* Richard Rodriguez actually recounts what he "did on his summer vacation"—but with such insight as to make his account a ready contrast to most students' work. Other fine personal essayists include George

Orwell, E. B. White, James Baldwin, Joan Didion, and Annie Dillard.) Acknowledge the terms that your students use in response to this question and—as appropriate—translate those terms back into the language of inquiry, so that students can see what the personal essay has in common with other difficult sorts of writing.

Some Possible Writing Assignments

- A paper entitled "One Thing I May Have Been Doing on My Summer Vacation That I Was Not Aware of at the Time"
- A paper entitled "One So-Called 'Fact of Life'"
- Chapter titles for an autobiography—one chapter title for each phase or aspect of the student's life to date—with a note added to each title, indicating what other titles the writer considered and why the writer settled instead on the title selected.

Teaching Idea 20: The *Big* Paper

Many teachers of writing see a bigger, longer paper as the fitting culmination of their courses. Some courses I myself have taught have been designed to build up to a final, ten- or fifteen-page research paper that calls into play in one project all of the various skills fostered by earlier, shorter assignments—a resounding symphony to follow mere sonatas and trios.

I am still compelled by the logic of such course design. To pull it off, however, requires knowing and neutralizing two strong tendencies of students: the tendency not to choose questions that will sustain them—questions, that is, that will continue to interest and engage them for the duration—and the tendency to leave the bulk (or even all) of the work involved to the last days or hours available.

The Right Question

One might naively suppose that since inquiry itself starts with forming a question, question formulation should come early in a course *about* inquiry. I have slowly come to feel, however, that that skill (strangely enough) generally surfaces late in the day.

Perhaps there is an analog in learning to drive. Until one has mastered the skills required for operation of a car—and achieved some *comfort* behind the wheel, a confidence to "go wherever"—one is not likely to have turned one's mind to the naming of new, ambitious destinations, like the Yukon or Yucatán; they seem beyond reach. Similarly, good, hard questions may seem out of reach—and therefore not worth contemplating—to the person who has not yet sensed his or her capacity for inquiry, for "getting somewhere" with the mind.

In the meantime, while my students are still *growing* sure in inquiry, I supply them with a long list of questions from which they can draw to supplement questions that occur to them personally. Here are half a dozen of those questions:

> What is there about American society that makes baseball America's "national pastime"?
>
> Discuss the belief that great literature of the twentieth century lacks protagonists who qualify as heroes. (Among the works you discuss, include at least two of the following authors: Anton Chekhov, Virginia Woolf, Ernest Hemingway, F. Scott Fitzgerald, James Joyce, Gabriel García Márquez, Chinua Achebe.)
>
> Is there intelligent life elsewhere in the universe?
>
> What is time?
>
> Identify the likeliest actual effects of a voucher system on the quality of public schools.
>
> Do human beings have free will?

Most of the questions on my list (which appears in its entirety on my Web site) are difficult *factual* questions, as opposed to moral questions; they qualify as difficult because the facts being sought in them remain unknown or uncertain. However, some of the questions on my list are difficult *moral* questions, requiring reference to values, as well as to factual considerations. The use of a long list of questions mixing types—and, within the factual type, freely crossing traditional disciplinary lines—reinforces an important tenet of my whole course: namely, that good inquiry always involves certain basic procedures of the mind, regardless of the content.

How, then, to encourage students to select questions for long papers that will sustain them? No doubt, diverse ways exist. For my part, I have each student submit to me a list of five questions, all of which must first pass muster in their minds for real felt interest and for real felt difficulty. What I tell them is: (1) "Every question must matter to you," and (2) "Every question must appear to you to be so hard that you are genuinely not confident of finding a definite answer to it in the time between now and the day when your paper is due."[4]

If the course I'm teaching is not thematic in nature, I invite my students to draw from the questions listed on my Web site—but only for one or two of the total of five questions. (In a thematic course, I would replace that list with another, more appropriate list, but I would always oblige students to generate most of their five questions without recourse to any list provided.)

Although I make it clear that I retain a veto power, I have students rank-order their respective lists of questions, to indicate their preferences. On some occasions, I fail to find any good question on a student's list of five and turn the whole list back for additions.

Pacing

Left to their own devices, few students will spread out the work of writing a long paper so as to maximize both their enjoyment of the process and the quality of their finished products. Consider naming milestones along the way and attaching a deadline to each milestone. (One such plan, The Building Sequence, is presented in the "Five Sequences" section near the end of this book.)

Also, time permitting, consider having one or two conferences with each student during his or her work on the project, to assess progress and to give your advice and support.

Inquiry and Service Learning

A student may be introduced in class to theories about homelessness or aging or illiteracy; out on the streets (or in shelters or community centers), he or she will see up close the situations which those theories purport to explain, and very few theories account for all particulars.

▶

Even if students derived nothing else from service learning (and, of course, many derive a great deal from it), the chance to test hypotheses against "facts on the ground" would justify continuing such programs and offering our students the option of including service learning efforts—as appropriate—in their big projects.

A Optional Preliminary to the Big Paper: The Statement of Difficulty

Few of the steps listed in the Building Sequence for producing a big paper (page 107) will surprise my reader. One, however, is unusual: the Statement of Difficulty, which is yet another means to get students to acknowledge complexity and uncertainty, and to deal with both states of affairs less fearfully. Here is the assignment itself, straight from an old handout:

> You should aim in this paper not to give me the answer to your question—not even tentatively or in brief—but rather to *present and explain* the question and to *show me that it's difficult.*
>
> Ironically, few students have been encouraged by their teachers to admit and demonstrate difficulty. In fact, the vast majority of questions you write on at school are very tough; scholars have pondered these matters, argued about them, and still failed to settle them once and for all.
>
> Admissions of difficulty are valuable: they tell us that a problem isn't as simple as it may at first appear—or as others would have us believe it is—and thus free us from our misconceptions. In showing us *why* a problem is difficult, admissions of difficulty actually move us in the direction of correct solutions; they break a problem down, identify those aspects of it which require further, better thought.

▶

Say that you have chosen the question, "Which energy source is to be preferred, nuclear fission or coal?" You might find the question hard to answer for numerous reasons. If you weighed only real, recorded casualties, coal—with its history of mine disasters and black lung disease—would seem the more hazardous of the two. If, however, you were also to consider possible future disasters, like meltdowns or explosions, and probable illness which has yet to manifest itself, like forms of cancer, the scales in your head might tip against fission. Contemplate the factual difficulties: How can one accurately *gauge* the chances of nuclear catastrophe, or of long-delayed cancer? (As was clear in the wake of the Three Mile Island incident, even experts on the matter bitterly disagree.) Or consider one of the ethical problems involved: At what point is a possible death sufficiently probable that it should count as heavily as real, past deaths do?

And so far, in your treatment of fission and coal, you would not have touched on: relative supply, economic costs, environmental implications not related to health, or any of various other relevant issues. (In breaking down a difficult matter into its difficult parts, you may suddenly realize that you can narrow the question and *still* fill your Big and Preliminary Papers without padding. Here, you might narrow to the question, "Which energy source *costs more in human life*, nuclear fission or coal?")

My point is this: Earth does not lack for tough problems. We do the cause of inquiry no service in pretending they're *not* tough. At least in your Preliminary Paper, *dwell* on difficulty.

Outcomes of Such a Course

Calling students' close attention to their inborn powers of inquiry; presenting them with questions of true difficulty, then supporting them as they begin to grapple with those questions. . . . What results does this approach to teaching writing yield?

Student thinking, by and large, becomes more honest, more extensive, more complex.

There was the pitcher on the Bentley College baseball team who went from writing a paper—on the question "What is time?"—that seemed drawn out and vacuous at just three pages, to writing a thirty-five-page, often-confused but rich and penetrating train of thought on the same question. There was the daughter of a nurse who, pondering on paper whether praise was good for children, suddenly realized she had possibly misunderstood the chapter on her subject in a book by Haim Ginott, therefore looked at it once more, then returned to her thinking—not just with a better reading of Ginott—but with a sharp distinction between *sorts* of praise, which drove her inquiry much further.

There were the students who in September sought my approval for their every idea—and by Thanksgiving needed to be told by me that I might have a thing or two to say on their subjects myself. (Only at that point would I *offer* my two cents worth.)

Here are excerpts from a better-than-average train of thought on global warming. (One section of this forty-six-page train of thought is written on toilet paper, proving, I suppose, that at least some students eventually come to agree with me that inquiry occurs everywhere.)

> Is man really destroying the ozone layer? If so, will partial destruction be as bad as people say?
>
> . . . first I'll take on the first question for a while, then I will take on the second, considering the first one must be proven for the second one to be relevant. . . .
>
> ---
>
> OH OK. trying to pin down exactly what the ozone layer *is* and what it *does.* . . .
>
> ---

do all gases mix?
I don't know—ask Steve.
he didn't know. . . .

. . . how could it be concentrated ozone if the stuff mixed?

well let's see—

exhaust from a car is a gas . . . once you get away a little bit from it the smell dissipates. . . .

so I guess the gases do mix. . . .

[four pages later] NOW WE ARE REALLY COOKIN'. . . .

I'm going to have to go to the library. . . .

	CL	+	O_3	
	^		^	
	chlorine		OZONE	MIX
to form	CLO	+	O_2	
	^		^	
	chlorine monoxide		oxygen	

O H Y E A H ! ! ! !

I can't believe I was right! and then the CLO + O2 take the place of the O3 and they don't do the same job, therefore we get HOLES in the OZONE LAYER!!

Hold on—how do I know that this is true? . . .

Notes

1. If memory serves, I owe this distinction to a debate between Peter Elbow and David Bartholomae at the 1993 Conference on College Composition and Communication.
2. My reader may object that inquiry is far more involved than this. How, for example, does one *come by* hypotheses? By what various means does one *do* testing? However, to characterize inquiry with any thoroughness goes well beyond the scope of this book. To learn why, for pedagogical purposes, the level of specificity to which I adhere in this model seems adequate to me, please see my note on pages 14–15.
3. Thanks to Joe Check of the Boston Writers Project for having introduced this exercise to me.
4. For a discussion of the types of theses available to students who don't reach simple, definite answers to their questions, see page 51.

II. Communicating One's Thinking

Teaching Ideas 21–25: Making the Transition from Writing-for-Thinking to Writing to *Report* One's Thinking

Teaching Idea 21: Taking a Stand against Pretending and Oversimplifying

The first crucial matter that needs settling when thinkers turn their attention to their audiences is whether to speak honestly.

I believe that what is true of me in this regard goes for most of my colleagues: We prefer a paper that fails to answer a question definitively—but reflects real grappling with that question—over any paper which has merely "taken a stand," *rushing* to judgment.

Take, for example, this excerpt from a paper in psychology:

> The first real problem that this question confronts me with has to do with the term "cross-cultural studies." It smacks so much of social anthropology that I begin to lose faith in my already precarious conception of psychology and what distinguishes it from other social and hard-core sciences. So I look to Brown and Herrnstein's introductory text for some guidance and the first line reads, "We may as well have the scandal out at once and get it over with: 'psychology' cannot be defined." The last puff of wind goes out of my sail.

A Harvard instructor gave the paper from which this excerpt is taken—a paper whose author more or less honestly attempts throughout to come to grips with a question, not pretending to know something she does not—the letter grade A.

Of course, honesty alone did not earn this student her A. She *worked* on the question assigned her, didn't give it just one glance, throw up her hands, and declare that she was confused. Also, she took pains to express herself in a well-ordered and clear manner. Honesty of judgment and hard work—work on substance and work at writing—these in combination earned her an A. That is as it should be.

We as teachers can take various measures to counter the reductive tendencies that students display when transforming their thinking with an eye to readers:

- For one thing, we can correct their misperceptions of their *current* readers—*us.*
- We can also inform them of types of thesis statements they have never used, as in the handout shown in Figure 4.
- We can also give students practice in spotting thesis statements that do not do justice to the richness of the writer's thinking on her subject. When a member of the class has produced a good, extensive train of thought, we can have students read it and formulate alternative thesis statements based on it, then choose among three or four such statements the one that best captures the nature and the fullness of the headway made in that train of thought.

If you prefer, in lieu of a train of thought by one of your students, you can use the set of thoughts and notes on alcoholism to be found on my Web site under "Organization Challenge" (discussed below). Those thoughts and notes purposely do not come with any adequate (i.e., faithful, comprehensive) statement of thesis, and deriving such a thesis from them makes challenging work. (Again, my Web site address is http://www.ncte.org/books/59133/resources/.)

- Additionally, we can help our students to *enlarge their repertoires of organizational and syntactical forms*, lest they avoid making *true* reports of their thinking just because doing so would (they fear) exceed their linguistic know-how. (See pages 55–56 and 69–71 below for specific teaching ideas.)

Must a Paper's Thesis
Be the Statement of a Simple, Definite Position?

Usually, no.

Most teachers at the college level want students to practice intellectual honesty and rigor, not just to "pick a side and defend it." They want students to discover the *complexity* inherent in difficult questions, and to deal with that complexity.

When the true end result of inquiry is a simple, definite position, that should be the thesis of one's paper. When, however, the true end result is something short of that, one's thesis should differ accordingly.

Fortunately, there are many ways to report one's progress on a question clearly, interestingly, and coherently, even when that progress points to an answer which is complicated or uncertain. A few examples:

- If the question at hand is, "What caused the Civil War?" one might demonstrate that the question *needs clarification.* One might write, "If 'cause' here means essentially the same as 'ignite,' then perhaps the election of Abraham Lincoln can be said to have caused the Civil War. If, however, 'to cause' means 'to help in any way to bring about,' then . . ."
- Or, one might demonstrate that *one possible answer should be eliminated.* One might write, "It would then seem that, while we cannot say what did cause the Civil War, the issue of slavery did not cause it—at least, not by itself."
- One might *speculate,* saying, "Have we, I wonder, taken sufficiently seriously the possibility that it was the North's tone of moral superiority, as much as the Northern position, that inflamed the South? An examination of rhetoric, North and South, reveals . . ."
- One might even *demonstrate one's own confusion.* One might write, "Historians identify no fewer than seven causes of the Civil War. Probably, each cause played its part, and so the question boils down to one of degree: Which of the causes mattered most? Unfortunately, though, determining a single cause's relative importance is almost impossible where causes are as intertwined as in this case. For example . . ."

Figure 4: Handout on types of thesis statements

Teaching Idea 22: Organization Challenges

Many students know no pattern for shaping prose beyond the famous Five-Paragraph Theme, that model which assumes a single, simple proposition and a stock of facts that line up neatly in support of it. By contrast, few of the questions worth asking in this world yield reports of progress quite so tame—when the thinking has been honest and extensive, and the thinker *reports* his or her thinking honestly.

I tell my students how I feel about the Five-Paragraph Theme and assure them of my confidence that they are capable of more than that. Then, to start to demonstrate my confidence in them, I hand each one of them a set of thoughts and notes on a difficult question—each thought or note appearing on its own three-by-five index card—and challenge them to put themselves in the place of the hypothetical student who, having recorded those thoughts and notes, needs to arrange them in the best possible order for a paper.

Myself, I use the set of cards on alcoholism to be found on my Web site: http://www.ncte.org/books/59133/resources/. Several of these cards are shown in Figure 5.

Before students begin the activity, I issue the following warnings:

1. The hypothetical writer *may or may not* have written out an explicit thesis statement yet. If you don't find one, you will need to formulate one that is faithful to the writer's thinking before proceeding any further. (Blank index cards are provided for you to fill in missing parts of the paper.)

   Likewise with a conclusion.

   As always, beware of oversimplification.
2. Since the writer's thoughts did not come to the writer in the same order in which they will need to be presented, there appear few or no transitional markers indicating how thoughts and notes relate to each other and to the writer's thesis. Write directly onto cards to insert such markers where needed.
3. One or two cards in the set may not even be relevant to the question the writer is addressing. These, you should discard.

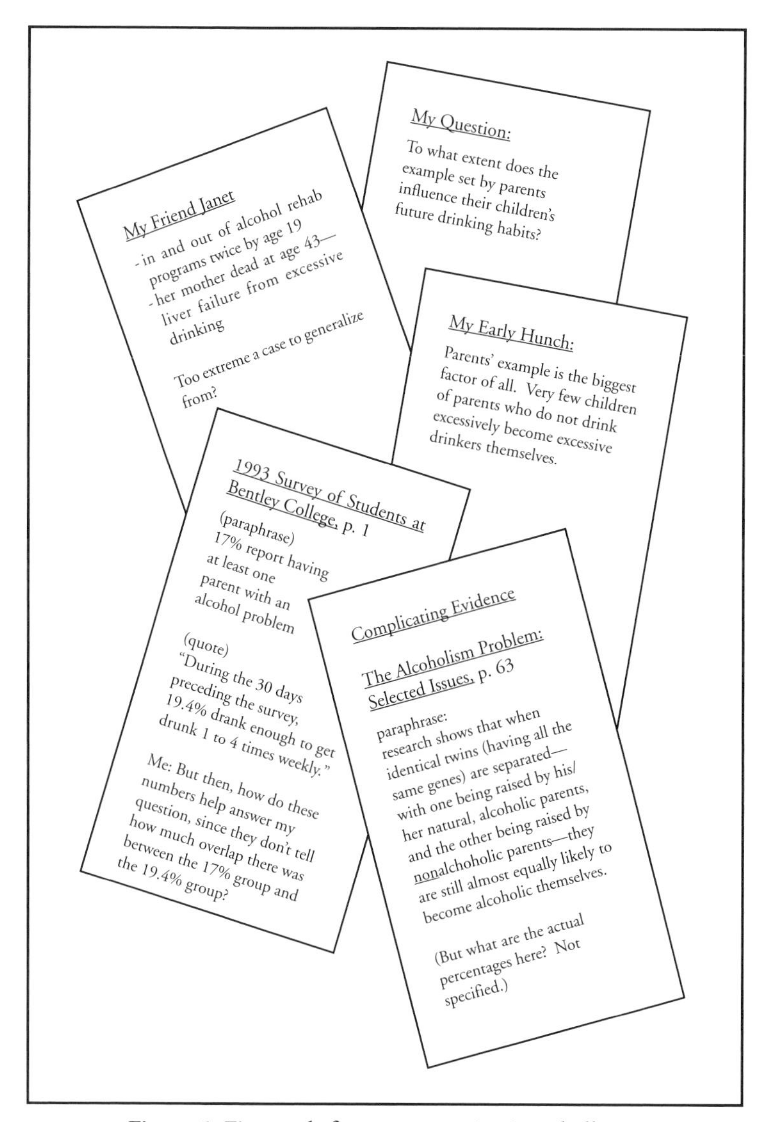

Figure 5: Five cards from an organization challenge

When my students have laid out their respective sets of the same cards, I invite two or three to say how they went about doing so, and then I give all of them some good, well-wrought *alternative* solutions to ponder. I rarely need to inject any judgments of my own in the discussion that ensues. Invariably, (a) some students are surprised that *anything* coherent can be made of the material, and (b) nearly all students—even those whose own ways of shaping the material would serve readers fairly well—duly note that there appear to be either comparably good or better prose designs available.

Teaching Idea 23: An Organization Checklist

One way to break the hold of the Five-Paragraph Theme—and so accommodate complexity—is to replace that much-too-simple model with a checklist. If the checklist is thoughtfully compiled, students using it will come to see that many diverse outlines qualify as sound. Here, for what it may be worth, is my checklist:

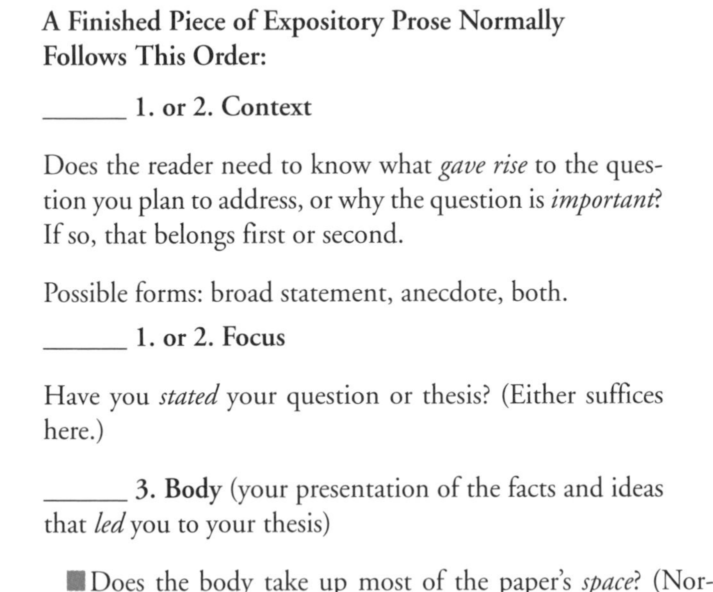

A Finished Piece of Expository Prose Normally Follows This Order:

______ **1. or 2. Context**

Does the reader need to know what *gave rise* to the question you plan to address, or why the question is *important*? If so, that belongs first or second.

Possible forms: broad statement, anecdote, both.

______ **1. or 2. Focus**

Have you *stated* your question or thesis? (Either suffices here.)

______ **3. Body** (your presentation of the facts and ideas that *led* you to your thesis)

- Does the body take up most of the paper's *space*? (Normally it would.)

- Have you broken the body down into its logical *parts*? Will your reader be able to tell how each part *differs from all other parts*?
- Have you put those parts into some logical *sequence* (temporal, spatial, least important to most important, least controversial to most controversial, etc.)?
- Will your reader be able to see how each part *relates to your thesis*?
- Have you left space to deal with possible *objections* to your thesis, either by concession or by refutation?

______ **4. Conclusion**

Do you end in a way that *ties your paper together without being simply repetitive*?

Possible forms: a thesis statement (if, for Focus above, you relied just on your question); a reformulation of your thesis; a new anecdote; a follow-up to or echo of the anecdote used above for context (making a frame around the paper); further implications of your thesis; further work needing to be done on your question.

This checklist appears also on my Web site, where it can be downloaded for copying: http://www.ncte.org/books/59133/resources/.

To introduce students to the *use* of a checklist, have them employ it as an aid in evaluating particular outlines or particular whole papers. (I myself would first let students issue their evaluations in any terminology that comes to them. Only then would I point them to the checklist and ask them whether in the checklist they find language for elaborating further.)

Teaching Idea 24: A Menu of Types of Organization

Another good way to break the hold of the Five-Paragraph Theme is to name and spell out *multiple* common forms of organization.

Five years ago, I enlisted undergraduate peer tutors at the Bentley College Writing Center to join me in determining and describing the organizational designs of hundreds of pieces of published expository prose and model student papers from around the country, in order to identify the organizational forms most widely used today. What emerged was a taxonomy somewhat different from those presented in handbooks I had read. We learned that the vast majority of shorter-than-book-length pieces could be categorized as using one of the following approaches:

- list
- setup/rejection
- comparison
- narrative
- hybrid (some combination of two or more of the above)

The booklet that resulted from this project, entitled *Blots*, appears in modified form on my Web site: http://www.ncte.org/books/59133/resources/.

Regardless what taxonomy you choose, you might reinforce your students' understanding of it with a lighthearted challenge: Have them, on the spot, concoct several alternative outlines (each outline representing a different organizational form) in response to the immortal question *Why did the chicken cross the road?*

You will not be disappointed.

A Not-So-Incidental Use of Knowledge of Organizational Forms: Improving Reading Comprehension

I never understood that literacy itself is bound up with organizational sense until, some twelve or thirteen years ago, I took some turns teaching Bentley College's noncredit course in speed reading, which had for its text a book of reading selections edited by Allan Sack and Jack Yourman (1981).

While I believe that the taxonomy of organizational forms introduced above (and spelled out on my Web site) ▶

will serve students better than the one of Sack and Yourman, Sack and Yourman's central point holds true: The reader who has learned common patterns used in shaping prose will both *get what she wants* from prose faster than other readers will (since she knows where to look for it within a text) and *comprehend writers' whole arguments faster* (since she knows how parts generally relate).

You and your students can test this claim in an exercise adapted from Sack and Yourman:

- When students appear to have mastered the several organizational forms you've presented to them, divide your class into two halves. To the students on your left, give five minutes' time to read a certain article or chapter. To the students on your right, do the same—and with the same article or chapter—but stipulate that at least the first two minutes (of the five minutes total) be spent determining how that article or chapter is organized.
- At the end of five minutes, have your students put their texts away, and give the following brief, ungraded quiz:
  - With what question is this author dealing?
  - What gave rise to this question in the author's mind? (Or, Why is this question important to the author?)
  - How does this author respond to the question?
  - What reasons and/or evidence does this author cite as basis for that response?
  - What, if any, concessions or exceptions does this author make?
- Go back over the questions in class, so that students can mark their own answers.
- Tally the results for each side of the class separately, and ask, "*What do these results suggest for reading practice in the future?*"

Teaching Idea 25: Putting It All Together

When I add a new element to my tennis game—say, "playing the net"—practicing that element itself, in isolation, is essential, but it's not sufficient. Whether in tennis or in chess or in writing, time must be made for taking newly learned skills and integrating them with preexisting skills, until the new and old fit seamlessly into the same, larger, more complex activity. To help students integrate skills of thesis formulation and organization with skills of inquiry, I do as follows:

1. I conduct a new Think Tank (pages 15–24) and follow up that Think Tank with an Interview (pages 24–25)—with this one addition: As a student recounts his inquiry to me, I stand at the chalkboard and write his thoughts—as well as the facts that he cites—on the board. Then I do the same with one or two other students.
2. Of the two or three sets of thoughts and facts I put up on the board in this fashion, I select the one which seems richest to me and declare that set to be our basis as we move into the organizing phase of writing, so that all class members have the same material with which to work. I ask everyone (a) to compose a *thesis statement* true to the thinking reflected in that set and (b) to create the topic sentence outline for a *whole paper* true to that set.
3. I then call three students up to the board to write their sentence outlines there for all to see, and have them underline their thesis statements.
4. About each of these outlines in turn, I ask . . .
   - Does the thesis statement faithfully reflect the sort of headway represented by the set of thoughts and facts? (For one thing, does it avoid oversimplification?)
   - How well would this plan of organization serve the needs of a reader? (It might serve one type of reader well; another, poorly.)
5. Having gone through all three outlines this way, I ask how they might be classified by *forms* of organization (list, setup/rejection, comparison, narrative, hybrid, etc.), and I label them

accordingly. Then I ask whether any class member has produced a sentence outline belonging to a type not represented on the board yet.

6. If, in the end, certain significant organizational alternatives are left untouched in this process, I respectfully add them myself.

Three viable alternative outlines for a paper on William Carlos Williams's poem "The Red Wheelbarrow"—all based on the same train of thought (see pages 16–17)—can be found on my Web site: http://www.ncte.org/books/59133/resources.

Teaching Ideas 26–28: Teaching Drafting

Teaching Idea 26: Banning Outlines, Dictionaries, and Grammar Handbooks

Perilous indeed is the moment when a student tells herself that she must now sit down and "write" her paper. If, by "write," what she has in mind is just to "follow her outline," merely adding two or three sentences for each point found there as she gets to it, the result is quite likely to be textual deadweight for the reader. Similarly, if she means to produce one essentially correct sentence after another—debugging every sentence for grammar, word choice, and spelling before setting her hand to the sentence that comes next—the result is quite likely to be flat.

Textual vitality depends partly on *flow* of expression, and flow, it may go without saying, is hard to achieve when a writer conceives writing as the filling in of blanks on her outline or as the meticulous creation of one flawless sentence after another. When writing flows, the writer dwells in what John Trimble (in his *Writing with Style*) calls "warm, imaginative touch" with her audience (1975, 19), exercising her good instincts for rhythm—and for saying next what it would be most helpful to a reader to be *told* next.

All too aware of the delicacy with which the post-outline moment needs to be approached by a writer, I . . .

- urge students to think of writing as a form—albeit a crafted form—of human speech;

- have them give their outlines one last look, and then have them put those outlines out of sight until they finish their initial drafts (a tack harder to take with fifteen-page papers than with three-to-five-page papers);
- emphasize that first drafts are rough drafts, and banish dictionaries and grammar books for the duration;
- and tell them of the practice (introduced to me through an essay by Linda Flower and John Hayes) of "satisficing" while drafting—the practice of quickly bracketing the words, phrases, and whole sentences that may need fixing or replacing later on, but refraining from that work (revision) for the time being, and moving on instead (1980, 41–42).

I attempt, in other words, to activate the oral (or discursive) instincts and to mute the fear of incorrectness. The attempt involves: (a) holding notes, plans, and outlines to the back of the mind, (b) placing dictionaries and other reference books well beyond reach, and (c) having problems merely noted in passing, rather than addressed as they arise.

Teaching Idea 27: Letter Writing Instead

Letters, it seems to me, occupy a curious niche on the continuum from speech to formal writing. To be sure, they are produced through fingers rather than through lips, but they pass between people familiar to each other and, therefore, they appropriate many of the features of real-time conversation.

In my experience, some students whose writing lacks fluency make strides in that regard when I invite them to think of the first draft of a paper as a *letter* to me. I suggest that they open with some line like, "Larry, you ask where all my reading and thinking on my topic has taken me thus far. Well, . . ." I implore them to "talk it to me" on the page. I assure them there will be time enough for lopping off their salutations and for fixing things up sometime later.

Other good openers include these writing prompts drawn from a longer compilation by my former colleague Sheila Reindl:

> When I started this course/paper/project, the thing that really interested me was . . .

The questions I find myself thinking about these days are questions like . . .

One of the things that makes my question a tough one to reckon with is . . .

I want to know . . .

I have a hunch that . . .

I wish I could say in my paper that . . .

If things were as neat and tidy as I'd like them to be, . . .

I'm stuck. I'm stuck because I can't figure out . . .

What stands out to me about all the stuff I've been reading is this idea that . . .

What I've been reading makes me wonder . . .

I'm learning that . . .

If you and your students are properly wired, you might have them correspond with you by e-mail.

Teaching Idea 28: Freewriting

Do you feel that in order for your students to attain greater flow in their expression in papers, they would need considerable, frequent practice outside the paper-writing process itself? Probably today's best known regimen for boosting fluency—although it has purposes besides that—is the practice described by, among others, Peter Elbow: freewriting (*Writing Without Teachers* 1973, 3–9).

In its pure form, freewriting has but one rule: Write continuously—taking ne'er a break for thinking or revising—for ten whole minutes. Do not let that pen—or cursor—stop even if you find yourself saying, "I have nothing to say. I have nothing to say. I have nothing to say." The faith on which freewriting rests (a faith borne out sufficiently often to warrant the continuation of the practice) is that the channels that connect the mind and the writing hand will soon be opened by this means.

A variant approach is to set students' freewriting going with a stipulated opening phrase. For freewriting about the topics of course papers, the prompts of Sheila Reindl above do nicely. As less directive openers—nets for the "daily catch," as it were—I submit the following lines and phrases:

As I sit here, . . .

Something which has been on my mind lately is . . .

Only _____ weeks left before semester's end . . .

I'd rather be . . .

Don't talk to me about . . .

What I admire is . . .

There are two sides to every story.

Some things don't change.

Who would have guessed it!

Let your students freewrite in the first ten minutes of class time—or have them do it daily at home. Again, if you and your students are properly wired, you might have them do it via e-mail.

(To keep to a minimum the time and effort that you give to *responding* to your students' freewriting, see page 98–99 below.)

Teaching Ideas 29–38: Teaching Revision

Teaching Idea 29: Encouraging/Requiring Revision

After they have learned that "making a mess" is a normal part of writing (a normal part of drafting, as well as a normal part of prewriting inquiry), students do need to learn that revision is a normal part of writing also! Many teachers . . .

- require that students bring drafts of papers to class, to *show that drafts exist by certain dates*, or
- let students *rewrite graded papers*, on the understanding that good revisions will bring changes of grade in their wake.

Myself, I do the former. In addition, though, near term's end, I require that each student revise one paper he or she has had marked and returned by me—not just revise it for mechanics, but substantially revise it, for a separate grade. I also ask that each revised paper have appended to it a statement of the writer's aims in revising.

Teaching Idea 30: Giving It a Rest

The first thing for a draft to do when it's complete is to absent itself—to hide away in a drawer somewhere, and not to come out again until its author no longer has on the tip of his tongue the things he had intended to say in it. Only then is he reasonably well positioned to play the first-time reader of his words, spotting . . .

- phrases that would *lack* meaning to a reader,
- phrases that can mean *more* than one thing, and
- claims that a reader would find unconvincing.

To make this point, have your students turn their first rough drafts of one assigned paper directly in to you. Then just blithely sit on those drafts for a few days before returning them unmarked and giving your students ten or fifteen minutes in class to do the marking themselves. Would they have seen as much need for revision on the day they turned their drafts in?

Teaching Idea 31: Eye Exercises

When (ideally, after "giving it a rest") students pick up a draft to revise it, some can spot its deficiencies in argument, some can spot the words in it that lend themselves to misreading, some can spot all of its grammatical mistakes, and so forth. Few, however, see *every* type of writing problem it contains.

I am here to say that many students' eye for such things can be sharpened as follows:

> Pull from your files five or six old student papers that are densely packed with problems of all sorts.
>
> Retype the first page of each so that no marks by you appear on it.

Distribute to your students the first page of the first paper and challenge them to mark and label all the problems to be found there.

When they have made an end of marks and labels, give them copies of the same page *with your exhaustive marks added.*

The unmarked and marked versions of one sample student-written page are shown in Figures 6 and 7. Do you need more? An unmarked set of six—which includes the sample reproduced here—appears on my Web site: http://www.ncte.org/books/59133/resources/.

Obedience to Authority

Creon infuriated by Antigone's betrayal for the burial of her brother Polyneices, faces his neice to discuss her situation. Antigone is betraying Creon because she has to bury her brother even though Creon specifically forbids it. Through discussing Antigone's father Oedipus, who killed his father and slept with his mother, Creon tries to anger Antigone. Antigone responded to this by saying she was leaving to bury her brother.

Creon tried to convince Antigone that a burial by a priestly abracadabra would not put her brother to rest. Antigone understands what Creon is saying, but she must put her brother's body to rest, so her brother is no longer humiliated.

Figure 6: Unmarked beginning of a student essay

Lead a discussion addressing these questions:

- What marks of yours don't all your students understand?
- Have any students "outdone" you, making marks that do not correspond to any of your marks? (Some of these, you may wish to *add* to your marks. Even we teachers' eyes can use sharpening.)

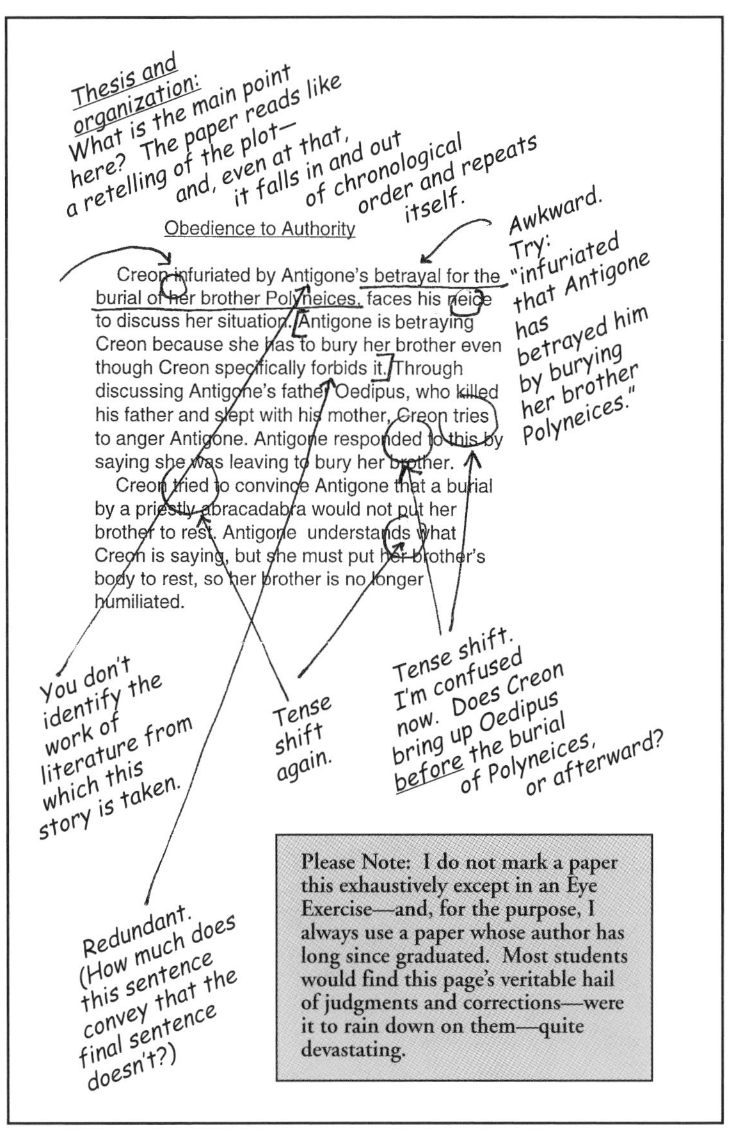

Obedience to Authority

Creon infuriated by Antigone's betrayal for the burial of her brother Polyneices, faces his neice to discuss her situation. Antigone is betraying Creon because she has to bury her brother even though Creon specifically forbids it. Through discussing Antigone's father Oedipus, who killed his father and slept with his mother, Creon tries to anger Antigone. Antigone responded to this by saying she was leaving to bury her brother.

Creon tried to convince Antigone that a burial by a priestly abracadabra would not put her brother to rest. Antigone understands what Creon is saying, but she must put her brother's body to rest, so her brother is no longer humiliated.

Please Note: I do not mark a paper this exhaustively except in an Eye Exercise—and, for the purpose, I always use a paper whose author has long since graduated. Most students would find this page's veritable hail of judgments and corrections—were it to rain down on them—quite devastating.

Figure 7: Marked beginning of the essay

- Point out to your students that some people "see" grammatical problems but do not "see" weaknesses of argument; others "see" disorganization but do not "see" vague or ambiguous word choice. Then, assure your students (which is true for most of them) that they can markedly improve their "eyesight" in revision if—in repeating this exercise several times with different student-written texts—*they self-consciously look harder for the types of problems that have eluded them (as individuals) initially.*

- Give them precisely that opportunity: Using the other first pages you have prepared, either conduct an additional four or five "eye exercises" in class, or let students do them on their own at home.
- Finally, have students submit all of their marked pages, along with a note assessing how much progress they have made as diagnosticians.

Teaching Idea 32: The Mutual Aid Society

When students are at work revising a paper . . .

- Have each student identify two revisions (other than mechanical corrections) he or she is contemplating making *that may not yet go far enough toward solving the writing problem at hand.*
- Have each student prepare two "before-and-after" sets of materials—one set for each of the two revisions under consideration. In the case of a changed plan of organization, the set would consist of an outline of the paper as originally submitted and a new outline. In the case of revised text, the before-and-after set would consist of one or two paragraphs of the paper as originally submitted, and one or two paragraphs intended to *replace* those paragraphs.
- Have each student make enough copies of his or her two before-and-after sets to provide all members of the class with a copy of each.
- In class, have each student take a turn . . .
  - distributing the copies of one of her or his two sets,
  - explaining what she or he *aimed* for in making the revisions,
  - and eliciting response. (Is the new version actually better than the original? Does it go as far as it *could* toward achieving the writer's aim?)

You, as instructor, should withhold your response until other class members have spoken.

Teaching Idea 33: Revision "Cells"

Once your students have grown sharper at *spotting* writing problems (by such means as the Eye Exercises discussed on pages 63–66) and savvier about revision *strategies* (through, for example, The Mutual Aid Society, directly above), they should be ready to start serving as writing consultants to each other without your leading them. By this point, they should be ready for revision "cells"—groups of between three and five students, all of whom take turns submitting drafts for comment by their fellow group members before submitting final drafts to you.

Mind you, the fact that you refrain from leading these cells yourself is not tantamount to your disappearance from the scene. Most all-student small groups encounter certain pitfalls; we teachers have roles to play accordingly.

- *Certain group members dominate*—but you can appoint one member to be official timer and charge that person with ensuring that each member of the cell gets equal time to share a draft and to preside over members' critical discussion of that draft.
- *Certain groups lose their way*—but at least in the beginning you can have cells meet in class time, so that you can circulate among them, listening in and reorienting them as necessary.
- *Some group members tend to rely too much on themselves; others, to rely too much on the group*—but you can announce that your evaluation of each paper will, as it were, be an average of (a) the grade its writer would have gotten on the draft he or she submitted to the group and (b) the grade the writer would have gotten on the paper in its final form. Each student would thus have incentives to be serious about the work in *both* its phases: the solitary and the consultative.

Teaching Idea 34: The Lighter Side of Imprecision

> One should not aim at being possible to understand, but at being impossible to misunderstand.
>
> —Quintilian

Once revision has begun, high on every good writer's checklist is the matter of precision: Do the writer's words bear only the meaning he or she intends them to bear, or could they be misread? If I err pedagogically when I address the issue of precision, it is on the playful side I err:

> I bring two neckties into class. I give one to a student who knows how to knot a necktie and one to a student who does not, and I have these students stand with their backs to each other. Then I ask the knowledgeable student both to knot his necktie and to give a running account out loud of what he is doing. I ask the other student to try to knot a necktie *based on the first student's description.*
>
> Before the actual knotting of neckties commences, I instruct all the bystanding students to make mental notes of the junctures, if any, at which communication breaks down. What specific utterances of the first student produce unfortunate results? Why?
>
> Almost without exception, the necktie of the second student soon becomes a mangled object of amusement. I ask all present how we could have been brought to such a pass, eliciting as much as possible of the language used by the first student. Factors identified typically include:
>
> - steps assumed and skipped,
> - terms whose meanings in context are vague or ambiguous, and
> - unclear pronoun references.
>
> More important to me than the identification of such factors, however, is the more general point: The fact that a writer knows well what he means by his words can hardly be said to guarantee that his readers will. In fact, the mess made of a necktie in this exercise is but the visual representation of invisible messes produced all the time by inexpert (and expert) writers in the minds of their readers.
>
> Also, I divide the class into two or three teams and have one member of each team leave the room. From a nondescript brown paper bag, I then pull a strange-looking object—an eggbeater, for example—and challenge each team to write the perfect, unambiguous set of instructions for drawing it.

> That done, I call one designated "artist" at a time back into the room to render the unnamed mysterious object based on his or her teammates' *words*.

In addition, I collect and distribute humorous instances of ambiguity like these:

Classified Ads
Auto Repair Service. Try us once, you'll never go anywhere again.
Dog for sale. Eats anything and is fond of children.

Headlines
Juvenile Court to Try Shooting Defendant
Drunk Gets Nine Months in Violin Case
Milk Drinkers Turn to Powder

Descriptions of Accidents (from Insurance Forms)
I collided with a stationary truck coming the other way.
The guy was all over the road; I had to swerve a number of times before I hit him.

John Kenneth Galbraith's All-Purpose Letter of Recommendation
I cannot recommend this person too highly.

Yogi Berra
When you come to a fork in the road, take it.

I report that writing with too careless a hand—"writing with mittens on," my former colleague Henny Wenkart used to call it—often makes it hard for writers *themselves* to track their arguments.

Teaching Idea 35: Enlarging the Student's Repertoire of Devices

Ever since the 1970s, when widespread interest in transformational grammar started waning (leaving many articles and drill books in its wake), not enough attention has been paid to students' generally poor supply of linguistic devices for showing the relationships among facts and ideas.

My informal study of English prose reveals twenty-two types of sentences, or phrases, by function: alternative, assumption, cause, comparison, concession, contingency . . . and sixteen others. Yet the collected writings of a typical student contain instances of only ten or twelve, and the means used to set *them* up—like the phrase "for example," to signal exemplification—get used repeatedly, for want of ready options. Can it be that a certain student never has points to concede to the opposition? Can it be that another never needs to make assertions of a strictly contingent nature?

My reader may by now have glimpsed large implications here for any course aiming both at full thought and at adequate expression of full thought. Even the student who, through inquiry, discovers the complexity of her subject will, in the end, seem simple-minded if she confines her actual writing to a very few syntactical structures and phrasal cues. As Harvard University President Neil Rudenstine said in his letter of August 1995 to the Harvard Class of 1999: "Whatever your chosen field of study, you will not be able to proceed very far unless you constantly master new vocabularies, experiment with new forms of syntax, and try to see how precisely and sensitively your use of words can begin to reflect the very best movements of your mind and imagination operating at their peak."[1]

To help students fill their gaps in linguistic resources, I have created a chart of common syntactical and phrasal devices, listing each under the sentence/phrase type that that device most often indicates. Thus, under the heading "Cause," I list:

- Because
- Thanks to
- In light of
- Since
- For
- Left-branching and right-branching explanatory phrases beginning with "-ed" or "-ing" verbals (e.g., "saddled with debt" or "not realizing her own strength")[2]

For the entire chart, see my Web site: http://www.ncte.org/books/59133/resources/.

I have tried calling my chart a "toolbox," a "repertoire," a "palette"—the labels I affix to it seem not to stick. Because of its size and shape, it's been called "The Placemat" from the start. No matter; so long as students make good use of the thing, I let them call it what they like.

Use of It

There will, I hope, be more ambitious uses of the Placemat to come (I have been trying one out for two or three years now), but its basic use is simple: With a highlighting marker of one color, each student marks all the devices that belong to his or her active repertoire already—i.e., all the devices which the student feels naturally "come" to him or her when needed. (Most students do quite well at this; I have randomly checked some self-assessments against actual papers by the self-assessors.) Then, giving special attention to devices under sentence/phrase types for which *no* devices have been highlighted, the student uses a marker of another color to highlight devices (limit of ten) that he or she would like to *add* to his or her active repertoire. The student keeps the marked Placemat out in view while revising papers, as a jog to memory.

Teaching Idea 36: Naming One's Models of Style

By and large, students don't wish to write prose which is formal and stuffy, but they do aspire to "maturity" of style. Ask them what in their view qualifies a style as mature, and you will (eventually) hear some or all of the following:

- It is more than simple sentences strung together. It demonstrates that the writer has the verbal wherewithal to handle complexity.
- It flows.
- It bears the stamp of personality—to the extent that the writing task at hand *allows* for that.

Having, through discussion, put into the air criteria like those above, give each student a sampling of diverse model excerpts from student papers, all of which pass muster for maturity of style, however much they also differ stylistically. Then, as a short, ungraded assignment, have each student (a) name the one, two, or three excerpts he feels most inclined to emulate and (b) try to deduce from that selection (doing no more oversimplifying here than for any inquiry) what specific stylistic features would rank high among his own desiderata.

A Note to Myself

(Containing, it may be, one or two good leads for you, my reader)

When all is said and done, I still don't do as much with style as I'd like to in my classes. I do nothing, for example, with prose rhythm. Also, I have yet to make good use of the ideas in two of my favorite books on writing: Herbert Spencer's *Philosophy of Style* (1959) and Walker Gibson's *Persona* (1969).

Teaching Idea 37: Ben Franklin's Exercise

The student who seeks a stylistic breakthrough in her writing can be invited—either for extra credit or in lieu of another assignment—to do some rounds of the regimen that that old self-improver Ben Franklin once devised for himself. I have freely adapted a section of Franklin's *Autobiography* (16–17) to come up with the following instructions for students:

DAY 1

Browse in the anthology of prose readings I have lent to you until you find a short passage—no more than 150 or 200 words in length—which you like quite a lot. Reduce that passage to a set of notes, using index cards.

- Every fact and every idea found in the passage should appear on a separate note card.
- Every note should be written in your own words, not the words of the published original.

Shuffle the note cards and put them away.

DAY 2

Look through your note cards.

Write the best passage that you can, based on your notes.

Only after you have written your own passage should you pull out the published original again and compare the two.

On a separate sheet of paper, write a brief appraisal of your passage as compared with the original. In what respects is the original a more effective piece of writing? In what respects is *your* passage more effective? What details of organization or style seem to account for these differences?

Teaching Idea 38: The Secret of Life

When students glimpse the vistas in writing skills development beyond "good work" and "competence," curiosity begins to stir in them about the means available for traveling to such new destinations. To the extent that it is "life" they want—writing that has "life" to it—they begin to ask what life's *ingredients* are: "How did Didion do that?" "How did Updike do that?"

I, for my part, play the shameless mountebank at such inviting times. I announce that I've identified the features present in all prose that is said to be lively, and proceed to unveil my findings as an equation:

Weinstein's Formula for "Life"
$L = 3V + E - C$

I, of course, let my students guess what all the terms of this equation represent, but for *your* information . . .

- the *L* stands for *life;*
- the *3V* for *vividness, variety, and voice;*
- the *E* for *economy;*
- and the *C* for *clichés.*

In addition, however, I announce my discovery of a simpler, *alternative* equation:

$L = A \ldots$

where *L* stands for *life* again and *A* stands for *attitude*. I explain that outcomes just as good or better than the ones achieved through the first equation can be achieved through the second—that is, simply through adopting a new *frame of mind* as a writer, a sense of oneself as "part entertainer."

Apropos of this second equation, I like to read my students the following excerpts from a letter I received in 1977 from my brother Warren Weinstein, in response to the draft of an essay that I'd written. Students tend to appreciate these excerpts on several levels at once.

> To be uncharmingly blunt, your essay just ain't funny enough—or, which is really more to the point, it isn't *pleasing* enough. I might also add, if you and God can ever forgive me for such an unfair generalization, that all your essays suffer somewhat from this shortcoming. . . . In this essay, for instance, I could only find one example of your when-you-want-to-be-buoyant style—*and that in apologetic parentheses!* . . . What are you apologizing for? Why are you so reticent to see the essay as a form of entertainment?
>
> If I may be so presumptuous, I myself would like to suggest a possible answer to this rhetorical question: your damnable profession. You are in the business—a dirty business, but someone's got to do it—of bringing college students down from their happy cloud castles of fluffy verbiage and billowing generalizations. It is your unromantic job to teach those hormone-ridden adolescents that the English language is a form of communication, rather than a mere effusion of sounds. To achieve this desired result, this replacing wind with earth, many ugly maneuvers are no doubt required on the part of the expository writing teacher—including perhaps that most desperate one of insisting that students write in *plain English*. But—and this is the point I want to make—even at those times when the teacher is forced to recommend such rhetorical abstinence, he should never try to fool his students (or himself) into thinking that such abstinence is anything more than a necessary and *temporary* evil.

> Despite what Flesch and Strunk and Newman and most of the other modern grammarian gurus preach, plain English is not the paradigm or summit of good prose. Rather, it is the base camp—that necessary level we must climb before we can gather our strength and enlarge our lungs for the trek above.

Feel free to quote my brother to your own students, if you like. Alternatively, I suspect that certain sections of Richard Lanham's outrageous book *Style: An Anti-Textbook* (1974) would serve the purpose just as well.

In the end, let the pudding stand as proof. Give students a "good," "competent" passage of student prose and challenge them to make it even better by "giving it life." (Tell them not to be inhibited by ignorance. Where, for instance, vivid details are lacking, tell them to concoct some.) At least in the hands of certain students—those typically most willing to share the fruits of their labors afterwards—the greater vitality of the text will be unmistakable and memorable.

Teaching Ideas 39–43: Dealing with Grammar

At least three arguments can be advanced against using class meeting time for instruction in grammar. First—as regards students whose grammar is poor—formal in-class instruction was, in all likelihood, the very pedagogical mode that failed to do the job in the first place.

Secondly, by the age at which our students come to us, they present numerous different grammar "profiles." One student may never use apostrophes, never join two independent clauses appropriately, nor consistently put quotation marks on the right side of a period. The student in the very next seat may do all these things, but may repeatedly create awkward and confusing sentences through lack of parallel structure and misplacement of modifiers. Consequently, most of what efforts we might make in class to address Student A's grammar problems would have no or little interest to Student B, and vice versa.

Finally, there is the alarm sounded both by David Bartholomae, in his essay "Inventing the University" (1985, 158–62), and by Richard H. Haswell, in his more empirical study "Error and Change in College Student Writing" (1988)—but perhaps put most eloquently by Mike Rose, in his *Lives on the Boundary*:

> As writers move further away from familiar ways of expressing themselves, the strains on their cognitive and linguistic resources increase, and the number of mechanical and grammatical errors they make shoots up. Before we shake our heads at these errors, we should also consider the possibility that many such linguistic bungles are signs of growth, a stretching beyond what college freshmen can comfortably do with written language. In fact, we should *welcome* certain kinds of errors, make allowances for them in the curricula we develop, analyze rather than simply criticize them. Error marks the place where education begins. (1990, 188–89)

And yet we cannot stand by and do nothing for deficiencies in grammar. As I have told hundreds of students over the years, one pays dearly for piddling errors. Often their price is confusion. Even more often, however, the price a writer pays for being ungrammatical is not the loss of meaning, but the loss of *ethos*[3]—the loss of readers' good regard for the writer as a credible source. Whether or not, on the reader's part, the writer's errors actually result in confusion, each successive error will *distract* the reader, fleetingly turning the reader's attention from the writer's content to the fact that the writer has erred. After two or three such distractions, the reader will commence to take from them a (quite possibly undeserved) impression of the writer as a person who is careless generally, and so discount the value of the writer's thought. "If the writer hasn't tracked his tenses," readers seem to say, "how can we assume that he has tracked his *subject's* ins and outs?"

As Lisa Delpit (1995, 152–66) and others have argued, we can no more ignore this reality when teaching students who speak a nonstandard dialect of English than we can when teaching imperfect speakers of the *King's* English.

Here, then, are specifications for a new curriculum in grammar for students in college or the last years of high school:

1. It should result in students' mastery of more of the rules of grammar. However, . . .
2. It should not proceed as the traditional, straightforward (lecture-style) curriculum has done.
3. It should accommodate students' diverse error "profiles."
4. It should inhibit a writer neither in his or her creation of first drafts nor in his or her use of new syntactical forms.

I try to meet these "specs" in the following ways . . .

Teaching Idea 39: Grammar Self-Assessment

Various handbooks come with diagnostic instruments. Find one such instrument you like—or write one yourself—and have your students use it. The instrument that I use, which I designed with help from tutors at the Bentley College Writing Center, tests only for twelve of the most common types of grammatical errors. It appears on my Web site: http://www.ncte.org/books/59133/resources/.

WWW

Provide your students with the correct answers, and then have them juxtapose those answers with their own.

Field your students' questions. (Be prepared to discuss gray areas—like the placement of a comma before the "and" that introduces the last item in a series, and the use of deliberate fragments from time to time.)

Finally, *have each student transform his or her self-assessment results into a personalized checklist*—not for use during the generative and rough-draft phases of writing, but for reference in the process of revision. My version:

The Twelve Most Frequent Errors in Grammar and Punctuation at Bentley College[4]

Error	Relevant Sections in Your Grammar Handbook
_____ Fragment	[In this column I refer my students to sections of their assigned handbook.]
_____ Comma Splice	
_____ Comma Missing Between Independent Clauses	
_____ Comma Missing After Introductory Clause or (in Some Cases) Phrase	
_____ Misuse of Semicolon or Colon	
_____ Comma Missing to Set Off Interrupter	
_____ Comma Missing with Nonrestrictive Clause—or Comma *Inserted* with *Restrictive* Clause	
_____ Apostrophe Error	
_____ Quotation Error	
_____ Unparallel Structure	
_____ Number Shift	
_____ Misplaced Modifier	

Teaching Idea 40: "Giving Reason" to Error

As time and circumstance permit, try to help a student probe his confusion about a rule to get at his root misunderstanding.

Over the years, one young man's teachers repeatedly told him to stop writing run-on sentences. Unfortunately, though, they never scrutinized a sample of his run-ons with him and respectfully asked him *why* he would not want to break it into two free-standing units.

One of his sentences went something like this: "Boston's teams get close to winning championships but don't ever make it the whole way, they choke in the end." It's a run-on because the clause "they choke in the end" contains its own subject ("they") and its own predicate ("choke") and so should be treated as a sentence in its own right (or joined to the first part of the sentence by some means other than a comma). Through questioning, however, it became clear that this student *knew* he should not join two complete thoughts in the same sentence that way. He had written the sentence that way because he didn't *consider* "they choke in the end" a complete thought. If it appeared alone, he said, *"no one would know who 'they' was."*

What this student needed, of course, wasn't repetition of a rule he had already heard many times, but a chance to air his own understanding of the rule and to have it corrected (and to get his own intelligence acknowledged).

The phrase with which I name this teaching idea—"'Giving Reason' to Error"—comes from Eleanor Duckworth, who writes of a group of elementary school teachers who constantly "sought to understand the way in which what a child says or does could be construed to make sense." As she puts it, "They sought to give him reason" (1987, 86–87).

Much of Mina Shaughnessy's fine book, *Errors and Expectations* (1977), is devoted to the same cause.

Teaching Idea 41: Speaking It Instead

Occasionally, awkward constructions are the product of inordinate fears about writing, and about the rigor with which written, as opposed to spoken, language is judged. As a case in point, I offer these two utterances by a student who is a nonnative speaker of English.

Spoken
The employee felt guilty that maybe, if it wasn't for him, his partner would not have been laid off.

Written
This person I talked He's been with Wang for maybe 8 years. How he got hired was by someone who recommended him at Wang.

This young woman is typical of one subgroup of the student population—which includes many native speakers too—who have "good ears" for English but lack confidence and therefore trip themselves up on paper. With such a student, I read a problematic passage of his or her work out loud (or have the student do the reading out loud) and inquire, "Do your words *sound* right to you?"

Also, I explicitly urge such a student to *think* of her writing as "talking on paper." (See pages 60–62 above.)

Teaching Idea 42: A Spelling Self-Assessment for the Age of Spell Checkers

In the age of spell-checking features on computers, most of the spelling errors that survive (and they possess a fitness to survive at which Darwin himself might marvel) are the homonyms, the words like "its" and "it's," "bear" and "bare," which sound like other words but have different spellings and different meanings. One's computer software fails to detect incorrectly spelled words when they are homonyms, because homonyms are, after all, words in their own right. What to do? Just as with grammar and punctuation above, find or devise a good diagnostic test, then have each student take it and use the results of it to make a checklist of the errors to which he or she is prone.

The spelling self-assessment I developed with writing center tutors has this much wit (and special pleasure) to it: Thanks, in particular, to two or three mischievous tutors, many of the sentences use content which would initially put a student in mind of the *wrong* answer—for example:

> It [seems/seams] to me that Kelly's jeans are in some serious need of stitching.

That self-assessment appears on my Web site: http://www.ncte.org/books/59133/resources/.

Teaching Idea 43: Proofreading Backward

Typically, by the time a writer proofreads the final draft of a paper, he or she is so familiar with it that each sentence calls to mind the next one. Consequently, writers often fly right past the very errors proofreading is supposed to detect: words missing; words repeated; errors in spelling and punctuation that flow from hitting wrong keys, rather than from ignorance; etc.

In class on the day a paper is due—but before your students actually submit it—have each student do one extra round of proofreading, *this time from the paper's end.* That is, have each student proofread the last sentence first, the second-to-last sentence second, the third-to-last sentence third, and so forth, all the way backward to the paper's opening. Proofreading this way defeats the high speed bred of one's familiarity.

Shortly, those among your students who need to make this practice a regular part of their writing process will know who they are.

The Writer's Internal Monologue

Cognitive psychotherapists like Aaron Beck have claimed that we of the species Homo sapiens lead relatively happy or unhappy lives depending on the "lines" we hand ourselves about them. Try that thesis out in class. Give your students a list of the things which other students have been known to tell themselves when writing and have them make check marks by those that sound like lines in their own monologues.

Self-addressed lines on the list that I have used in class include:

> This could be interesting.
>
> I'm not sure I understand the assignment.
>
> I would like to write the "perfect paper" and to knock the socks off my teacher.
>
> I need to remember to break down big projects into smaller, bite-sized pieces.
>
> I can't get myself going.

▶

> I would be afraid to turn in a paper that expressed my own thoughts on this topic. I'm not qualified to do that.[5]
>
> In notes to you or in discussion, have students comment: What, if any, lines get in their way in writing? Where do these lines come from? Can such lines be stricken from one's script or changed?

Notes

1. Some, in fact, would go even further than this and claim that more than expression is involved: they believe that, without means for *expressing* complex thoughts, people are less likely to have those complex thoughts in the first place. "Thought," according to Vygotsky, "is born through words" (1962, 153).
2. The term "left-branching"—abbreviated LB on the full chart that is available on my Web site—refers to syntactical devices available for use in a sentence *before* the main clause. (The classic periodic sentences of Cicero lean heavy to the left.) The term "right-branching"—abbreviated RB on the chart—refers to syntactical devices used *after* the main clause. (Francis Christensen's "generative sentences"—like Faulkner's line, "She came among them behind the man, gaunt in the gray shapeless garment and the sunbonnet, wearing stained canvas gymnasium shoes"—lean heavy to the right.) Students unaware of all the options left and right will be able neither to pack as much into a single, graceful sentence, nor to manipulate emphasis as well as students with that knowledge can.
3. Aristotle's term, from *The Rhetoric*.
4. I advise my students to mark any type of error which they made two or more times on the self-assessment instrument.
5. For my whole compilation, please see my Web site: http://www.ncte.org/books/59133/resources/.

III. Two or Three Important Matters Not Yet Addressed

Teaching Ideas 44–46: Building Credibility

Teaching Idea 44: Setting an Example

A teacher of writing is ideally more than a "pronouncer" on writing: he or she is someone who writes and who deals in an ongoing way (albeit more effectively, most of the time) with the same writing issues confronting students. What is more, my ideal teacher of writing lays bare his or her process of writing for students' *inspection*.

Even as your students plunge into a written train of thought, let them—through the corners of their eyes—observe you "thinking out loud on paper" yourself, puzzling over the same question that confronts them, suddenly having a possible answer occur to you and noting it down (excitedly, if that's your style), and so on—all the while, being so absorbed by the problem before you that time's passage and your class's existence visibly recede from your consciousness. (It goes without saying that any student too absorbed by his or her own thinking to notice *you* in *your* mind's throes has no *need* of the example you are setting.)

On occasions when your students read aloud from trains of thought or rough drafts, take part. For a session of the Mutual Aid Society (see page 66 above), seek feedback on a true problem from *your* current writing.

The Example You Set by How You Refer to Books You Assign

Apropos of modeling, do not overlook the potential for modeling independent critical thought inherent in dramatizing (or at least reporting) your true feelings on the published works appearing on your reading list. No book that you might assign to students can perfectly accommodate your pedagogical aims. *Let students know where you and a book part company—even if it's just to say the author has devoted too much space to a matter of* little *importance, or too little space to a matter of* great *importance.*

Neglecting to take such pains, you might inadvertently give to certain students the impression that you're cowed by books yourself.

Teaching Idea 45: Guests Representing Students' Futures

Students have reasonable doubts about the claims a teacher of English makes concerning inquiry in general. Quite rightly, they wonder whether uses of the mind that apply to the interpretation of literature also apply to business case studies and physics experiments. Likewise, they are inwardly skeptical about an English teacher's claim that *writing* well is valued in this world outside of English courses.

Your credibility can be greatly enhanced by inviting into class guest scholars from different disciplines—as well as nonacademic people, such as police detectives and architects. As to inquiry, let each guest address questions like:

- What is your current project? Is it typical of projects in your field?
- On that project, what have you actually done to answer the question at hand (or to solve the problem at hand)? For example, did you wait until all the evidence was in before

venturing possible answers or solutions, or did you start hypothesizing early in the process? Where did your ideas come from? How likely is your final idea to be the same as your first idea?

And about writing, let each guest answer questions like those below:

For guests who are teachers . . .

- What do you most hope to see in students' papers? (If your guest has brought along copies of one or two papers she considers model papers, these can be her means to illustrate the virtues that she names.)
- Where do student papers most commonly go wrong?
- How important are mechanical matters—grammar, punctuation, spelling, and the like—in your evaluation of a student's writing?
- When a student is addressing a subject of true difficulty, involving complexity and uncertainty, do you prefer that that student's paper faithfully reflect that complexity and uncertainty, or do you prefer that that student's paper cut through all of that and take a definite stand?

For guests who are *not* teachers . . .

- What forms of writing do you do on the job?
- What percentage of your working time do you spend on writing? (Please take into consideration the time you spend putting your thoughts and data in order, doing the writing itself, getting feedback, and revising.)
- Which, if any, aspects of writing do your customers/clients or colleagues/supervisors care about? Can you recount specific comments made?

Be sure to leave time for students to ask questions before you pose questions of your own, and for you and students to debrief together afterward on the extent to which guests' answers corroborate or contradict the models of thinking and of writing promoted in class.

Teaching Idea 46: Memorable Quotes

On a day without a guest, you can still add to your own voice a second, credible one. You can write out a quotation on the chalkboard as your class assembles. It will get read; it will be pondered. I have assembled some favorite quotations on inquiry and writing for you to cull for possible additions to your own stock:

On Inquiry

Knowledge will come neither to the timid nor to the overconfident.

—An Arab saying

Every complex problem has a simple solution—and it's usually wrong.

—H. L. Mencken (attributed)

Getting it wrong is part of getting it right.

—Charles Handy

The practice and habit of writing not only drain the mind but supply it too.

—William Strunk Jr. and E. B. White

The trouble with bad student writing is the trouble with all bad writing. It is not serious, and it does not tell the truth.

—Eudora Welty

On Revising

There seems to be a sort of fatality in my mind leading me to put at first my statement or proposition in a wrong or awkward form.

—Charles Darwin

My wife took a look at the first version of something I was writing not long ago and said, "Dammit, man, that's high school stuff." I have to tell her to wait until the seventh draft, it'll work out all right. I don't know why that should be so, that the first or second draft of everything I write reads that way.

—James Thurber

Novelists . . . have, on the average, about the same IQ as the cosmetic consultants at Bloomingdale's department store. Our power is patience. We have discovered that writing allows even a stupid person to seem halfway intelligent, if only that person will write the same thought over and over again, improving it just a little bit each time. It is a lot like inflating a blimp with a bicycle pump. Anybody can do it. All it takes is time.

—Kurt Vonnegut

What makes me happy is rewriting. . . . [I]t's like cleaning house, getting rid of all the junk, getting things in the right order, tightening things up. I like the process of making writing neat.

—Ellen Goodman

Ernest Hemingway: "I rewrote the ending to *Farewell to Arms*, the last page of it, thirty-nine times before I was satisfied."
Interviewer: "Was there some technical problem there? What was it that had you stumped?"
Hemingway: "Getting the words right."

On Clarity

Vague and insignificant forms of speech, and abuse of language have so long passed for mysteries of science; and hard or misapplied words with little or no meaning have, by prescription, such a right to be mistaken for deep learning and height of speculation, that it will not be easy to persuade either those who speak, or those who hear them, that they are but the covers of ignorance. . . .

—John Locke

Everything that can be said can be said clearly.

—Ludwig Wittgenstein

> The difference between the right word and the almost-right word is really a large matter—'tis the difference between the lightning-bug and the lightning.
>
> —Mark Twain

> Words are like kisses—they can express everything or nothing.
>
> —Liz Glista, Writing Center Tutor

On Grammar and Punctuation

> Grammar is a piano I play by ear, since I seem to have been out of school the year the rules were mentioned. All I know about grammar is its infinite power. To shift the structure of a sentence alters the meaning of that sentence, as definitely and inflexibly as the position of a camera alters the meaning of the object photographed.
>
> —Joan Didion

> No iron can stab the heart with such force as a period put just at the right place.
>
> —Isaac Babel

Teaching Ideas 47–51: Two-Wayness, Part I—Students' Feedback to You

I don't recall what impelled me to do it, but near the end of the first course in writing I taught at the college level, I gave my students a list of statements about writing. Some of these reflected views of my own. Others were antithetical to views I held and espoused. My request of my students was simple: Would they, to assure me of my clear communication with them, please underline every statement they might reasonably attribute to me.

The results filled me with dismay. My students would have scored higher by underlining statements at random.

The state of affairs I now create in class—in which I listen to my students practically as much as I talk to them—I call "two-wayness." In it, learning is not assumed to be occurring just because teaching is occurring. On the contrary, learning is seen to depend on numerous unknown contingencies. Using this approach, a teacher views no given teaching method as surefire; instead (incidentally modeling inquiry for students in yet another way), he or she regards every class activity and every assignment as a *trial* effort. In order to determine whether he is "getting through" to students, he frequently has all of them talk *back* to him.

Teaching Idea 47: What You Would Say, What You Would Not Say

Try making a list like the one I refer to above: a list that mixes writing-related beliefs to which you subscribe and comparably fine-sounding beliefs to which you do *not* subscribe. See if your students can tell the difference. (Be sure to be sitting down when you peruse the results.)

Alternatively, have students do the Internal Monologue described on pages 81–82 above; then have them go through all the lines again, this time indicating which of them you, their teacher, would probably identify as signs of good writing practice.

Whatever modes of feedback you employ, follow up ASAP with new explanations or classroom activities, depending on the misconceptions or concerns that come to light.

Teaching Idea 48: The Reusable Feedback Form

At several points throughout your course, distribute a simple form like this one:

Feedback to Larry

1. Of the different things which have happened so far in this course . . .

   Which, in your opinion, are likely to contribute to your growth as a writer?

   Which, in your opinion, are *not* likely to do that?

2. Of the ideas presented so far, which leave you puzzled or unclear?

3. Other Comments:

Your Name (Optional):

When the feedback you elicit is discursive in nature—as it is here and in Teaching Ideas 50 and 51 (as opposed to Teaching Idea 47)—you do more than *ascertain* the actual effects of your teaching to date: you *consolidate* those effects, since, in being discursive, students must take what they have heard (or half-heard) from you and process it more actively. They must say it themselves. They must begin to imagine applying it.

Teaching Idea 49: Drawing Inquiry

Set out some enticing art materials for making black-and-white drawings, including: large sheets of paper (but none larger than your photocopier can copy), charcoal pencils, and felt pens. With these, have your students make *pictures* of what thinking—thinking for academic purposes—feels like to them. (Do certain students draw blanks, so to speak, when asked to describe such thinking in general? If so, have those students focus on the paper-writing experience which is freshest in memory for them.)

Some will turn out nothing more imaginative than my flow chart (page 13 above), but many will do better than that, even without your mentioning the various possibilities in advance (see Figure 8). A few will produce allegories—Kafkaesque as well as religious. A few will produce intriguing abstracts.

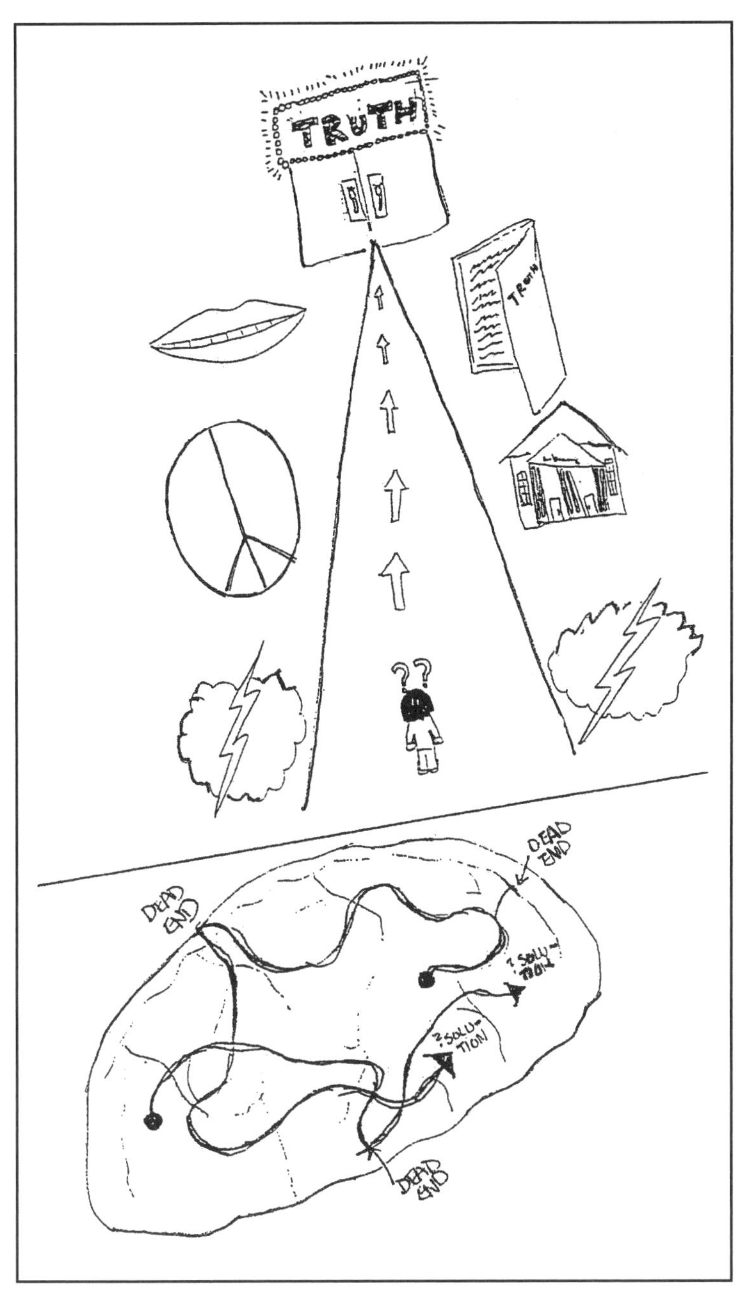

Figure 8: Two students' pictures of what thinking for academic purposes feels like

Copy and give to your students a representative sampling of these drawings and invite them (a) to ask questions of the different artists and (b) to reflect out loud on the sampling as a whole. (How do the visions of inquiry there square with each other? How do they square with the model of inquiry used as a reference point throughout the course?)

An activity like this permits you, among other things, to feature the work of students who are gifted visually but do not generally get much attention in a class where words are the coin of the realm.

Teaching Idea 50: Quotes of the Day—Milked

To vary things, on one or two occasions when you've tendered a quotation of the day (pages 86–88 above), get your feedback for the day in the following manner:

- As class winds down, refer—or refer again—to that quotation on the board. Perhaps, for example, on a day devoted to the nature of inquiry, it is:

    > Knowledge will come neither to the timid nor to the overconfident.
    >
    > —An Arab saying

- Tell your students that you need to know how well you have communicated your ideas to them, and ask them, in that context, to write notes to you saying either (a) what the quote of the day means to them personally or (b) what they suppose it means to you.

When, to pursue my example, I use the Arab line above, students have usually seen that "timid" might characterize the person who does not venture possible answers of his or her own, and that "overconfident" might well describe the person who asserts him- or herself *too* freely, stating possible answers as if they were final, not troubling to subject those answers to relevant tests. But students' other explanations for my choice of that quotation can be equally revealing and discussable.

Teaching Idea 51: Miscellaneous Feedback Prompts for One-Time Use

If you have gone at some key concept three or four ways but seen little return from your efforts, ask:

> As regards [here, name the dead horse you've been beating], have I, do you think, become too repetitious?
>
> If so, why do I observe so little change in this regard in class members' writing? (Maybe my ideas about this facet of writing are simply wrong! If you believe they're wrong, please tell me that.)

As you near term's end, ask:

> How, if at all, would you say that this course hangs together? *That is, what are its notable parts, and what do they have to do with each other?*

and/or . . .

> Of the different concepts and skills promoted in this course, which, if any, do you hope will "stick" with you in later life?

Teaching Ideas 52–56: Two-Wayness, Part II—Your Feedback to Students

Certainly, students need evaluative comments from us; they need to know whether we think they are "doing it yet." And certainly, by term's end, most of the schools at which we teach expect us to perform the teacher's gatekeeping function: the assignment of letter grades indicating students' differing degrees of readiness to do the writing tasks awaiting them in other courses or the larger world.

The use of letter grades entails high pedagogical costs, however. For one thing, the appearance of a letter grade on a course paper tends to draw the writer's attention away from the more substantive comments that we make. It also feeds the perception that we circle words and phrases—and write in the margins—not so much to inform or instruct the writer as to compute the writer's worth in letter-grade form.

I say "the writer's worth," rather than "the writing's worth," advisedly. The second high—actually, much higher— cost incurred in using letter grades is in students' self-regard. Because our students understandably *associate* an A, B, C, or D with gatekeeping, they attach it to themselves as much as to their products-of-the-day. They don't stop with saying, "This paper on Maxine Hong Kingston's *The Woman Warrior* was deficient in some ways, I suppose"; all too often, they go on to say, "I am just a C or C-plus student when it comes to writing, I suppose; I don't have a writer's gifts," and leave off trying for more.

With that in mind, I propose . . .

Teaching Idea 52: Keeping Letter Grades to Yourself

I myself now put no letter grades on individual papers. Instead, I provide feedback of other sorts (below) and record a letter grade only at my course's end, reflecting the student's work overall. As the course begins, I explain my reasons (discussed above) for this grading policy; as the course ends, I exhort my students not to take even their final letter grades too seriously, since (a) in department norming sessions my colleagues and I have sometimes been known to diverge in our evaluations of samples of student prose, revealing a subjective element in teachers' weighting of criteria, and (b) any student *can*, with some time and work, yet *learn* to write "A" papers.

In fairness to students in whom my grading policy initially creates anxiety, I invite members of my class to see me privately at any point to get me to translate their work to date into a grade. Typically, just one or two class members make that request of me—never more than three.[1]

Teaching Idea 53: Varying Your Feedback Roles

Even by the briefest of our comments in their papers' margins, students can make out the various distinct roles and voices we assume for the occasion of providing feedback to them. Sheila Reindl (in an unpublished 1995 essay) has named nine common respondent roles; Peter Elbow and Pat Belanoff, five. Here, I shall confine myself to three that cover the majority of cases: Judge, Doctor, and Reader. In each of Figures 9, 10, and 11, I name one of these roles and show how a teacher playing that role might mark a certain piece of student writing.

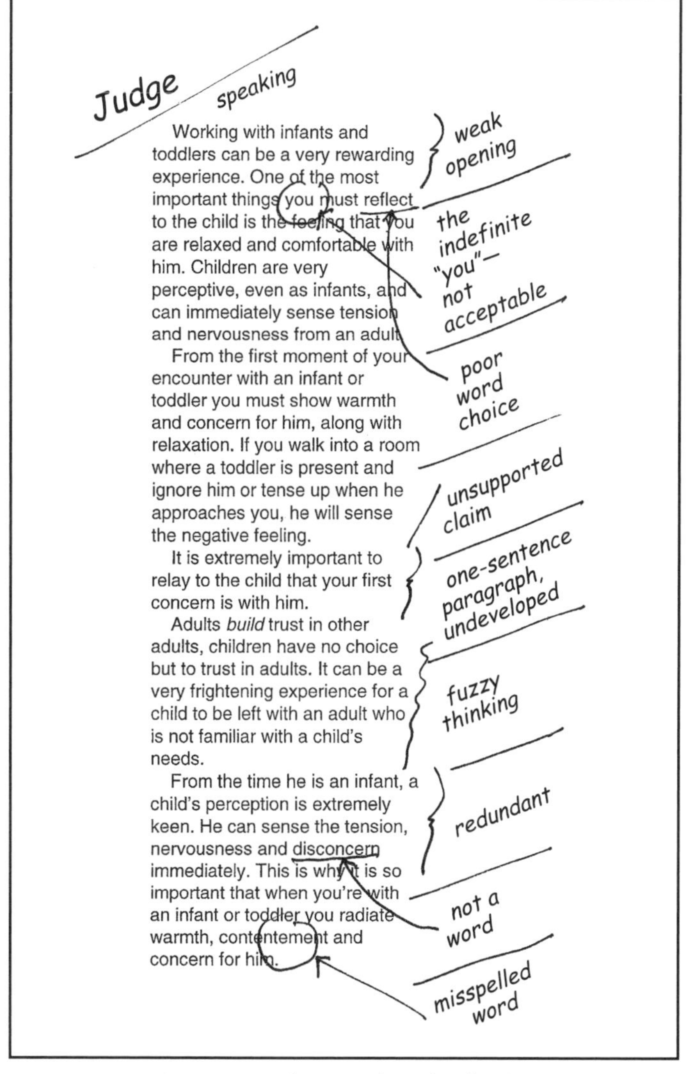

Working with infants and toddlers can be a very rewarding experience. One of the most important things you must reflect to the child is the feeling that you are relaxed and comfortable with him. Children are very perceptive, even as infants, and can immediately sense tension and nervousness from an adult.

From the first moment of your encounter with an infant or toddler you must show warmth and concern for him, along with relaxation. If you walk into a room where a toddler is present and ignore him or tense up when he approaches you, he will sense the negative feeling.

It is extremely important to relay to the child that your first concern is with him.

Adults *build* trust in other adults, children have no choice but to trust in adults. It can be a very frightening experience for a child to be left with an adult who is not familiar with a child's needs.

From the time he is an infant, a child's perception is extremely keen. He can sense the tension, nervousness and disconcern immediately. This is why it is so important that when you're with an infant or toddler you radiate warmth, conttentement and concern for him.

Figure 9: Marking in the role of Judge

With time, a teacher develops a sense for which of these voices to use with which students. Of the three, the Doctor is most directive, going so far as to name corrective action to take. Except with students who cannot be expected to possess any applicable knowledge concerning the writing problem noted—such as ESL students

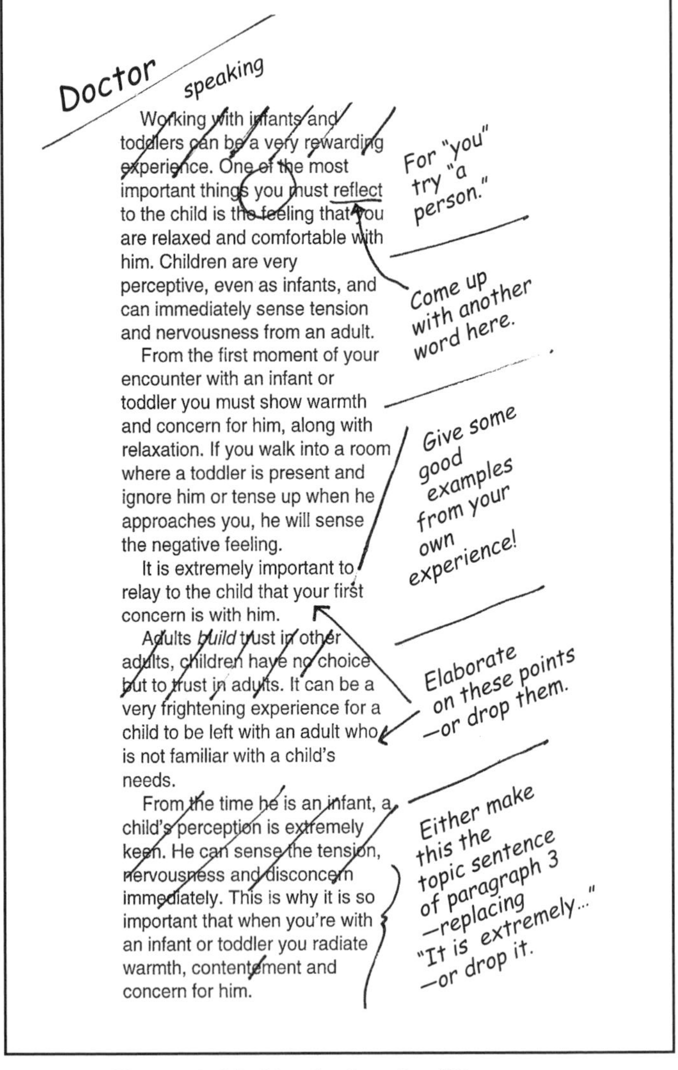

Working with infants and toddlers can be a very rewarding experience. One of the most important things you must reflect to the child is the feeling that you are relaxed and comfortable with him. Children are very perceptive, even as infants, and can immediately sense tension and nervousness from an adult.

From the first moment of your encounter with an infant or toddler you must show warmth and concern for him, along with relaxation. If you walk into a room where a toddler is present and ignore him or tense up when he approaches you, he will sense the negative feeling.

It is extremely important to relay to the child that your first concern is with him.

Adults *build* trust in other adults, children have no choice but to trust in adults. It can be a very frightening experience for a child to be left with an adult who is not familiar with a child's needs.

From the time he is an infant, a child's perception is extremely keen. He can sense the tension, nervousness and disconcern immediately. This is why it is so important that when you're with an infant or toddler you radiate warmth, contentement and concern for him.

Figure 10: Marking in the role of Doctor

making purely idiomatic errors—I eschew the Doctor role; students otherwise eventually depend on me to do revising for them.

As often as I can, I play my students' Reader, in which voice I try to make the real-world *costs* of miscommunication clear to them.

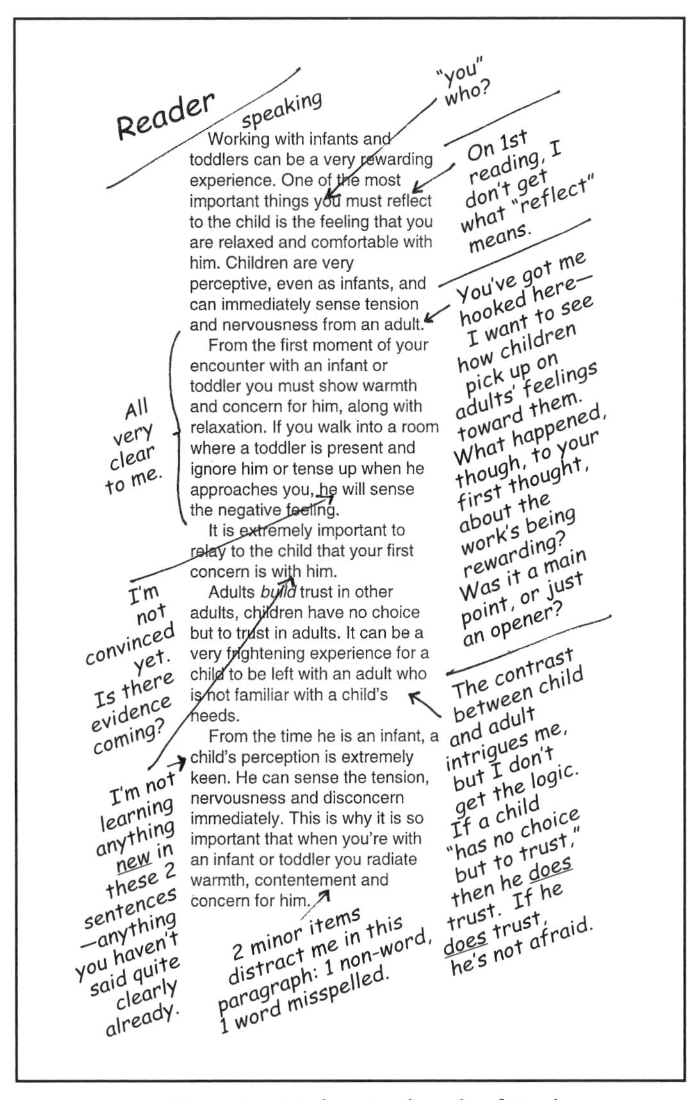

Working with infants and toddlers can be a very rewarding experience. One of the most important things you must reflect to the child is the feeling that you are relaxed and comfortable with him. Children are very perceptive, even as infants, and can immediately sense tension and nervousness from an adult.

From the first moment of your encounter with an infant or toddler you must show warmth and concern for him, along with relaxation. If you walk into a room where a toddler is present and ignore him or tense up when he approaches you, he will sense the negative feeling.

It is extremely important to relay to the child that your first concern is with him.

Adults *build* trust in other adults, children have no choice but to trust in adults. It can be a very frightening experience for a child to be left with an adult who is not familiar with a child's needs.

From the time he is an infant, a child's perception is extremely keen. He can sense the tension, nervousness and disconcern immediately. This is why it is so important that when you're with an infant or toddler you radiate warmth, contentement and concern for him.

Figure 11: Marking in the role of Reader

Teaching Idea 54: First Things First

Insightfully, Nancy Sommers warns us that we undermine our own frequent calls for "global" revision—for reconsideration of the merits of one's argument, for reorganization, for rewriting whole passages from scratch—if, in fact, we too early point out problems at the surface level, such as shifts of tense, misplaced commas, and misspellings. Understandably, from our attention to mechanical details, students infer that the portions of discourse in which those details are embedded must be worth preserving.

Two suggestions:

When you read first drafts of papers, make no marks for surface errors at all. Explain to students why such marking would be premature at this point.

Or—at the bottom of a student's last page, or on a separate sheet or special checklist—indicate the *types* of surface error that the student's draft contains, but provide few particulars, and those merely as examples. Urge the student to turn next to larger issues of revision, and to put off checking her whole text against your list of error-types until all larger matters have been dealt with.

Teaching Idea 55: Saving Time

No factor militates more powerfully against giving students additional practice in writing than the time it takes us teachers to respond to what they write. Therefore, consider both increasing your number of writing assignments and spending less time in responding to certain ones.

- For certain "small" assignments, confine feedback to some checkmarks on a photocopied list of your criteria.
- For certain other assignments, give feedback only to the class as a whole, not to individuals. Demonstrate that you have read students' papers by citing and reading out loud several excerpts that *illustrate* your general points. Or, when rapport and good humor characterize your relations with your class, occasionally make some fanciful awards to students, based on their papers: The Jackson Pollock Award for Unrelieved Abstraction; The One Memorable Sentence Award; and so on.

- For assignments involving numerous installments—like the assignment to keep a daily journal—check that the pieces exist, but read with care only those two or three the writer deems strongest or most interesting.

Teaching Idea 56: Postscripts

As teachers, we find ourselves bringing students the good or bad ("objective") word about their writing. We are the appointed bearers of society's high standards. If, however, we value the generally greater motivation to learn that comes when one tells oneself what needs improving, we should give our students chances to assess *themselves* as writers.

Probably the simplest form of self-assessment is the postscript. It is nothing but a brief, informal note tacked to the end of a paper (or draft), stating the writer's view of "where things stand" with the paper at the moment of submission: what it succeeds in doing; what, if any, problems with it yet remain.

When, after students have used postscripts to assess themselves, it comes time again for us to do assessing, we should, I believe, lay emphasis on the extent to which our students' judgments and our own agree. We should applaud whatever small or great self-critical acumen students have displayed and cheer them on. With a student's self-assessment for context, the same evaluative information that normally goes out negatively charged can be tempered with praise. Thus, "Alice, you need to learn to use transitions" becomes: "Alice, you have done a fine job of putting yourself in your reader's place. Your word 'choppiness' perfectly describes the impression that your writing sample made on me."

Note

1. Does this grading policy go too far for you? I was once enrolled in an outstanding seminar in versification taught by the late Robert Fitzgerald. Rather than affix a standard letter grade to each of our assignments, he would write one of the following: NTG (for "not too good"), NTB (for "not too bad"), NB (for "not bad"), or NAAB (for "not at all bad"). His marking practice had almost the same salutary effect that my marking practice has.

IV. Five Sequences: Ways to Design a Whole Course

What Remains to Be Done

Now that you have had an earful of my teaching principles and practical ideas for classroom use, all that I have left to share with you here is five different ways that a teacher might shape a whole course from such teaching ideas. In each of the five sections that follow, I present a different, quite distinct course plan—or "sequence"—for your consideration.

When all is said and done . . .

Like you and your students, I myself continue to need feedback. Please don't hesitate to tell me that I am on target in this book, or to set me straight. I can be reached at: Department of English, Bentley College, Waltham, MA 02452, or (781) 891-2918, or lweinstein@bentley.edu.

Once again, teaching materials can be obtained at the following Web site: http://www.ncte.org/books/59133/resources/.

WWW

The very best to you. LW

The Moratorium Sequence

A teacher would be justified in having serious misgivings about attending to students' *formal expression* of thought before hooking students on thought itself—open-ended, high-order critical and creative thinking. Despite good intentions, we often discourage true inquiry—a messy business at best—by rushing to correct for coherence, word choice, and spelling, even on Day One.

In several of my writing classes, I have now effectively put off my students' (and my own) attention to such matters of expression just by putting off all "paper writing" for a while.

The Moratorium Itself

Tell your students, "You will have much to write in the first phase of this course—things such as trains of thought, sets of notes, and journal entries—but no 'papers,' which are prohibited until further notice. *Our first concern is fullness of inquiry.*"

Use class time for the **Sizing You Up** and **Eavesdropping** teaching ideas (pages 5 and 6, respectively). Homework (ongoing until course's end) would be the **Reflective Journal** (page 12).

Then, use class time for **Think Tanks** with **Pulling for More** (pages 15–27). Homework: additional Think Tanks.

The Transition

Once you have provided students with an experience of fuller, more engaged thinking (and they are pleased with themselves as thinkers), proclaim a twofold aim for the balance of the course: to *keep* the mind-wheels turning, and to build skills needed for clearly and persuasively *reporting* the mind's work.

Ask your students, "In what ways does a good, extensive train of thought differ from a good paper?" Agree to points concerning redundancy, organization, diction, and the like, but resist any claim that seems to involve distortion or oversimplification, such as, "In a paper, you must take one side and defend it."

Use class time for **Putting It All Together** (pages 58–59), to demonstrate that even complexity and uncertainty can be rendered coherently and lucidly. Homework: "a paper based on your [the student's] most extensive train of thought to date."

The Return to Concerns of Expression

In class, give your reactions to your students' first papers, listing the aspects of their writing that need attention and laying out the rest of your course accordingly.

For instance, if your students' weaknesses as writers include disorganization, a lack of syntactical variety, and imprecision, you might proceed as follows:

- Use class time for **Organization Challenges** (pages 52–54). Homework: an alternative outline for the first assigned paper (even if that paper's organization was satisfactory).
- Use class time to have some students go to the chalkboard and write out both organizational plans—an outline of the paper as submitted, as well as the alternative outline. Ask the writer and the writer's classmates which plan is to be preferred, and why.
- Use class time for the **Placemat** and for the **Lighter Side of Imprecision** (pages 69–71 and 67–69, respectively). Homework: revision of the first assigned paper, especially for organization, syntactical variety, and precision.
- Use class time for a **Mutual Aid Society** (page 66). Homework: a further, final draft of the same assigned paper.

From this point to the end of the course—depending on the time available—you might shift to an abbreviated version of one of the other sequences in this series.

The Building Sequence

Here, several short papers prepare the student for producing a long, ambitious paper. They do so in two ways: by generating content that will appear in the last paper, and by introducing—one at a time—the types of inquiry normally *subsumed* in a big research project: summary, synthesis, and critique.

1. Warming Up and Choosing

- Homework: to choose a question for the **Big Paper** (see pages 42–44 above).
- Meanwhile, in class: Ask your students, "How do you imagine you will go about *working* on the question you select?" The closest they are likely to come to discussing *thinking* is to say, "Do research." Without evaluative comment by you, make a list of their responses on the chalkboard. Then, among other things, emphasize the need *to save time to think, probingly and extensively.* Use **Eavesdropping** and/or **Riddles** (pages 6–8 and 8–10, respectively), and/or one or two **Think Tanks** (pages 15–27), to set up and to clarify your statement of the differences between your students' conception of inquiry and your own conception of it. For good measure, throw in a **Flow Chart** (pages 13–15).

2. Dedicated Journal

- Once your students have settled on their questions, require them to keep a **Dedicated Journal** (page 13).
- In class: Have students make their first entries. Walk about to look at these (but look only at passages your students do not classify as being off-limits), and give more guidance, as needed.

3. Field Trip to the Library

- See the "**Field Trip to the Library**" section on page 30.

4. Summary

- Homework: to write a summary of one source to be cited in the big paper (pages 31–33).

5. Synthesis

- Homework: to write a synthesis of two other sources to be cited in the big paper (pages 33–35).

6. Critique

- In class: Pull one or two **Phonies** and/or have students **Write in the Margins** (pages 35–38 and 38–39, respectively).
- Homework: to write a critique of a fourth source to be cited in the big paper.

7. A Report on What Makes the Question Difficult

- In class or individual conferences: Check in with students on the progress of their thinking.
- Homework: to write a **Statement of Difficulty** (pages 45–46).

8. Drafting

- Homework: drafting the big paper (pages 59–60)—and **Giving It a Rest** (page 63).
- Meanwhile, in class: *Warn students that their big papers cannot be produced merely by stringing together passages from their shorter papers.*
- Also in class: Use class activities found in this book to highlight aspects of writing which—based on your reading of students' earlier papers—you believe they ought to bear in mind while writing their big papers.

9. Revising

- Homework: to revise the final paper before submitting it.
- Meanwhile, in class: Hone revision skills through **Eye Exercises** and **Revision Cells** (pages 63–66 and 67, respectively).

The "Amazing Disappearing Teacher" Sequence

The rationale for this sequence is simple enough. Ideally, all of your students will become more autonomous as writers. However, writing well autonomously entails mastery of skills that cannot all be learned at once. Through this sequence, a teacher *gradually* weans students off of their dependence on the teacher, handing students more and more responsibility for the writing task itself over time, as their mastering of skills proceeds.

In the sample case laid out here, the skills the teacher aims to gradually impart are those required for conducting good, extensive inquiry on research topics, but the principle involved can be readily applied in teaching such aspects of writing as organization, precision, and grammar, as well.

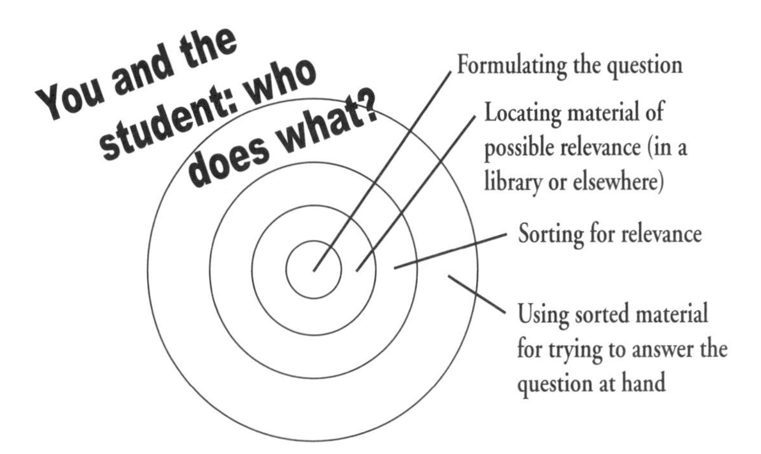

Let students know that the end result of your course is greater autonomy.

During Phase 1, supply your students with questions to address and with *research materials presorted for their relevance to those questions.* To your students themselves, leave "only" the task of thoughtful processing.

Appropriate class activities and out-of-class assignments include:

- **Sizing You Up** and/or **Eavesdropping** (pages 5–8),
- **Maker of the Rules** (pages 10–11),
- Distribution of a **Flow Chart** (pages 13–15),
- **Think Tanks** (pages 15–25), with **Tuneless Background Music** (page 27),
- and the writing of one or more short papers addressing questions posed by *you* and drawing from presorted, relevant research materials provided by *you.*

During Phase 2, continue to provide students with the questions to address and the research material that constitutes "grist for the mill"—but now mix mostly *relevant* material with some *irrelevant* material, and expect students to add the sorting function to the processing function, as their responsibility.

Appropriate class activities and out-of-class assignments include:

- **Guests** (pages 84–85), or
- and, again, the writing of at least one short paper.

During Phase 3, have students add to the processing and sorting functions the task of locating materials of *possible* relevance. Confine yourself to naming the question, and then set your students free with it.

(For at least one paper in this phase of the course, you might have students do both library research and another type of research—such as interviewing, observing, or experimenting.)

Appropriate class activities include:

- **Field Trip to the Library** (page 30), and
- yet again, the writing of at least one short paper.

In this sequence, only the targeted skills—here, skills of research—are held to a prescribed order. Other writing matters are taken up *ad hoc*, as in the Teachable Moments Sequence (below).

During Phase 4, tell your students that they are now on their own. Look to them to do not only all of the foregoing, but also to name their own questions, subject to your approval. (See "**The Right Question**" [pages 42–44].)

Another Application of This Sequence: Grammar

In Phase 1, decide which three or four grammar rules each student most needs to master, and make a list of these for the student. On a paper by the student, mark the first one or two errors of each listed type; then, for subsequent paragraphs, indicate the number of errors of each type to be found in each paragraph, challenging the *student* to find and correct the unmarked errors.

In Phase 2, refrain from all direct marking. Just indicate the total number of errors of each listed type to be found in the paper as a whole, and, again, leave your student to find and correct all the errors.

In Phase 3, put into effect a policy of "zero tolerance" for any of the listed errors.

The Individualized Sequence

It was from UCLA Professor of Education Gary Fenstermacher that I first heard of a course designed to accommodate students' different paces and styles of learning. Years afterward, I heard American Federation of Teachers President Albert Shanker opine that the best curriculum of all might be that which most closely resembled the Boy Scout Manual—stipulating skills to be mastered, but leaving the timing to students themselves, and offering students alternative means of achieving and demonstrating mastery.

Here is my—alas, as yet untried—syllabus for such a course. Readers of this book who try out the approach before I do are urged to contact me (c/o the English Department, Bentley College, Waltham, MA 02452; or lweinstein@bentley.edu), letting me know how realistic a syllabus this is, as well as what improvements might be made in it.

A Possible Course Syllabus

In this course I want to give you maximum possible credit for what writing skills you possess already and maximum possible credit for what skills you successfully master in the months to come.

To pass the course, you must submit at least the following pieces of writing, each at a passing level of quality:

- three short papers—each between three and five pages in length—chosen from
  - a summary of one of your assigned readings
  - a synthesis of two or more of them
  - a critique of one of them
  - a reflective personal essay
- one longer paper—between seven and ten pages in length—on a question either
  - chosen from a list of questions which I hand to you
  - or proposed by you and approved by me
- and a substantially revised version of one of the above papers, with a note describing and explaining your revisions.

To ensure that time exists for me to give comments on each paper—and for the writer to contemplate my comments before submitting his or her next paper—I require that no two papers be submitted in the same week.

However, beyond these requirements for passing, what grade you earn in this course is largely up to you.

Below I have listed the skills I consider most important in writing. After naming each skill, I have indicated the maximum number of points a student can earn by demonstrating mastery of that skill. For mastering a skill partially, a student earns the number of points which, in my judgment, reflects his or her *degree* of mastery. (Any student who would like to earn more points for a skill than I initially award is most welcome—urged, in fact—to try for it again, using either the same mode of demonstration or a listed alternative. Scores for first and second tries are not added together; higher scores replace lower ones.)

In determining course grades, I use the following scale:

C, for basic competence and effort to improve;
B, for 75–89 points;
A, for 90 or more points.

A Warning: Generally speaking, a student doesn't earn as many points as he or she desires on the first attempt to demonstrate a listed skill. *To do well in this course, it is therefore essential to start making such attempts early.*

☐ Skill to Master: Full, Extensive Inquiry

For a maximum of 20 points, either . . .

- keep a highly engaged Reflective Journal throughout the course
- or submit a Train of Thought in which you make real headway on a question of true difficulty.

(Confused? I will be explaining trains of thought and journals—and sundry things mentioned below—in class.)

☐ Skill to Master: Critical Reading

For a maximum of 10 points, either . . .

- find a serious, problematic article on a difficult question and produce a Dialogue in the Margins (often requires first photocopying the article to create large margins)
- or keep a Dedicated Journal on the reading that you do on a paper topic.

☐ Skill to Master: Organizing Complex Material Coherently

For a maximum of 20 points, either . . .

- submit a well-organized paper on a question of true difficulty*
- or create a new Organization Challenge, like the ones I sometimes use in class—and create three alternative solutions to the challenge.

☐ Skill to Master: Writing with Clarity

For a maximum of 20 points, either . . .

- submit a paper whose every word conveys only the meaning you intend by that word*
- or spot and correct the numerous problems of clarity in a set of Eye Exercises I present to you.

---

*One and the same paper can be used for credit for several of the skills listed here, but it is rare that on a single paper any student earns as much credit for all of these skills as he or she needs or wants. (All footnote markers in this discussion refer back to this thought.)

☐ Skill to Master: Writing in a New Style—Which You Yourself Determine

For a maximum number of points to be negotiated, depending on your aims, either . . .

- submit a paper written in the new style*
- or do three rounds of Ben Franklin's Exercise for Style.

☐ Skill to Master: Writing Correctly

For a maximum of 15 points, either . . .

- submit a paper in which not one of the twelve common grammar and punctuation errors occurs—and in which this effect is not achieved by relying too heavily on simple sentences*
- or do a Grammar Self-Assessment, and then submit a paper in which no more than two of those errors occur.*

☐ Skill to Master: Transference of the Skills Learned in This Course to Other Courses

For a maximum of 15 points, either . . .

- keep a Dedicated Journal in one of your other courses
- or submit a paper written for another course and append to that paper a note relating it to our concerns in *this* course.

Use of Class Time in the Individualized Sequence

At intervals throughout the course, have each student indicate the skills to which he or she would like to have class time devoted. Of course, in responding, feel free to draw on teaching ideas included in this book.

In conferences—or stretches of class time when other class members are occupied—check in with individual students who seem to be off to a slow start or to be struggling.

The Sequence of Teachable Moments

Arguably, what this approach lacks in "shape," it makes up for in immediacy—providing students with ideas about writing at just those points in time when they are liable to be most receptive to them.

In teaching by teachable moments, one assigns papers in any order that suits. Topics might, for example, move steadily from the personal and informal to the "objective" and formal. In deciding on the use of class time, however, one does not preplan; rather, one goes from one class session to the next, using class time in ways responsive to students' feedback forms (pages 88–93 above), in-class remarks, and observed writing weaknesses.

Here are some examples of how such teaching might proceed over a two-month period.

September 13

You conclude that most of your students' first extended trains of thought are little more than strings of bald assertions on the topic assigned, reflecting less true inquiry than you elicited from them when playing **Maker of the Rules** (pages 10–11 above).

Accordingly, in class you . . .

- point this out and ask your students why it should be so,
- concede that in Maker of the Rules the facts needed for testing assertions were supplied to them,
- use the chalkboard to format the inquiry at hand *as* a round of Maker of the Rules, and, in this way, press that inquiry further.

September 18

Noting that half of the class misunderstood an assigned reading, in class you . . .

- lead a **Power Summary** (page 33 above) of another text,
- and then do the same with a difficult passage of the assigned reading in question.

September 25

On a **Feedback Form** (pages 88–93 above), one of your students tells you that she feels you are "messing with her mind"—and, moreover, that her mind is not something that needs your attention, since it has served her "plenty well enough" in numerous classes at the high school level. You get her permission to share this reaction in class.

In class you . . .

- share the reaction, acknowledging its importance,
- invite comments of other class members,
- pause to absorb all that has been said,
- proceed to think aloud at length in your students' presence—in effect, *demonstrating* unafraid, honest inquiry—hypothesizing that your student was reacting to the self-consciousness necessarily involved at first in a course like yours, and that self-consciousness will pass when inquiry (a natural process, after all) starts "happening" more—but also testing that hypothesis with facts (including other class members' diverse reactions and the experiences of former students) and promising to return to this matter later in the term.

October 16

Although an excellent class discussion of a topic preceded students' writing papers on it, no student cited a classmate as a source of an idea in his or her paper. In order to foster more respect among students for their own and classmates' intellects, in class you . . .

- ensure that students know each other's names
- and require that in their next papers students credit at least two classmates by name, as sources.

October 23

Deciding that enough time has elapsed without attention to mechanics, in class you . . .

- distribute anonymous excerpts from papers which reflect good thought but contain errors of grammar and punctuation, to dramatize the needless cost in *ethos* (page 76 above)
- and administer a **Grammar Self-Assessment** to your students (pages 77–78 above).

October 30

In response to a student who justifies the one-sidedness of his papers by saying, "I would make concessions if I knew the ways that writers do that," in class you . . .

- acknowledge the difficulty of expressing complicated thoughts gracefully
- and point out readings which exemplify graceful concession making, as well as the array of concession-making devices on the **Placemat** (pages 69–71 above).

November 13

As promised on September 25, you follow up in class about "mind games." (Does inquiry still not feel like a natural activity to any members of the class?)

Works Cited

Bartholomae, David. 1985. "Inventing the University." Pp. 134–65 in *When a Writer Can't Write: Studies in Writer's Block and Other Composing-Process Problems,* ed. Mike Rose. New York: Guilford Press.

Beck, Aaron T. 1979. *Cognitive Therapy and the Emotional Disorders.* New York: Meridian Books.

Berthoff, Ann E. 1978. *Forming, Thinking, Writing: The Composing Imagination.* Rochelle Park, N.J.: Hayden Book Co.

Delpit, Lisa. 1995. *Other People's Children.* New York: The New Press.

Dewey, John. 1991. *How We Think.* Buffalo: Prometheus Books.

Duckworth, Eleanor. 1987. *"The Having of Wonderful Ideas" and Other Essays on Teaching and Learning.* New York: Teachers College Press.

Elbow, Peter. 1973. *Writing Without Teachers.* London: Oxford University Press.

———1987. "Closing My Eyes As I Speak: An Argument for Ignoring Audience." *College English* 49 (January): 50–69.

Elbow, Peter, and Pat Belanoff. 2000. *Sharing and Responding.* 3d ed. Boston: McGraw-Hill.

Flower, Linda S., and John R. Hayes. 1980. "The Dynamics of Composing: Making Plans and Juggling Constraints." Pp. 31–50 in *Cognitive Processes in Writing,* ed. Lee W. Gregg and Erwin R. Steinberg. Hillsdale, N.J.: Lawrence Erlbaum Associates.

Franklin, Benjamin. 1986. *Autobiography and Other Writings.* Edited by Kenneth Silverman. New York: Penguin Books.

Gibson, Walker. 1969. *Persona: A Style Study for Readers and Writers.* New York: Random House.

Haswell, Richard H. 1988. "Error and Change in College Student Writing." *Written Communication* 5 (October): 479–99.

Lanham, Richard A. 1974. *Style; An Anti-Textbook.* New Haven: Yale University Press.

Perkins, David N. 1981. *The Mind's Best Work.* Cambridge, Mass.: Harvard University Press.

Perry, William G. 1970. *Forms of Intellectual and Ethical Development in the College Years; A Scheme.* New York: Holt, Rinehart and Winston.
Rose, Mike. 1990. *Lives on the Boundary: A Moving Account of the Struggles and Achievements of America's Educational Underclass.* New York: Penguin Books.
Sack, Allan, and Jack Yourman. 1981. *The Sack-Yourman Developmental Speed Reading Course: An Analytical Method to Develop Reading Efficiency.* New York: College Skills Center.
Shaughnessy, Mina P. 1977. *Errors and Expectations: A Guide for the Teacher of Basic Writing.* New York: Oxford University Press.
Sommers, Nancy. 1988. "Responding to Student Writing." *College Composition and Communication* 32 (May): 148–56.
Spencer, Herbert. 1959. *Philosophy of Style.* New York: Pageant Press.
Trimble, John R. 1975. *Writing with Style: Conversations on the Art of Writing.* Englewood Cliffs, N.J.: Prentice-Hall, Inc.
Vygotsky, Lev Semenovich. 1962. *Thought and Language.* Edited and translated by Eugenia Hanfmann and Gertrude Vakar. Cambridge: MIT Press.

Author

Photo by Warren Weinstein

From 1973 to 1983, Larry Weinstein taught expository writing at Harvard University, where he became the first preceptor in charge of the Expository Writing, Theory and Practice course and co-founded the Writing Center. Since 1983, he has been a member of the English Department at Bentley College, where, over time, he has enlarged his repertoire of teaching ideas to address the needs of students whose writing abilities range more widely than those of Harvard students do. He loves to teach and earns high ratings from his students. Currently, he serves as director of Expository Writing at Bentley.

Weinstein is also keenly interested in writing instruction in the precollege years. While serving four elected terms on the school board of Cambridge, Massachusetts, he visited and sat in more than 120 classes (and self-published "Inside Classrooms in Cambridge," a report of his visits). He has led workshops for elementary-, secondary-, and college-level teachers in Massachusetts, New Hampshire, New York, Pennsylvania, Louisiana, California, and Washington.

The text for this book was designed and typeset in Garamond
by R. Maul.
The typeface used on the cover was Granjon.
The book was printed on 60-lb. Williamsburg Offset
by Versa Press, Inc.